TEEN SELF-ESTEEM

A Common Sense Path To a Happy and Succesful Life

Charles L. Van House, Sr..

Sarah M. Swoszowski, M.A.

Life Lines Press, Buford, Ga.

Teen Self Esteem

A Common Sense Path to A Happy and Successful Life

Published by:

Life Lines Press
6338 Ansel Court
Atlanta, Ga. 30518

Publisher's Cataloging in Publication
(Prepared by Quality Books Inc.)

Van House, Charles L., 1914-
    Teen self-esteem : a common sense path to a happy and successful life / Charles L. Van House, Sr., Sarah M. Swoszowski.
    p. cm.
    Preassigned LCCN: 93-091367.
    Includes bibliographical references and index.
    ISBN 0-9635745-7-4

    1. Teenagers--Life skills guides. 2. Self-respect. 3. Self-control. I. Swoszowski, Sarah M. II. Title.

HQ796.V35 1993   305.235
                            QBI93-349

What People Say About This Book

Young People:

I now realize what is important and not important. It's wonderful."--Natalie Reed, age 15.

"Cool, man, cool. Easy to read and interesting."--Jason Vaughn, Age 18.

Knowing where a relationship is going is a key skill I and other teens need.--Rob Allen, age 16.

Professionals:

"I enthusiastically endorse this book as being a valuable tool for building a happy, responsible life." -- Gloria Lee, Human Resources Consultant.

"This book was written from the heart and it speaks to teens in a language that is direct and understandable.--W. Beecher Duvall, Ed. D., public school counselor.

"Teens are seldom exposed to such large amounts of 'common sense.' Teens, parents, and counselors will find it worthwhile reading. The book could be read without discussion, but, perhaps with more impact if discussed in small groups led by an appropriate adult facilitator." -- George M. Gazda, Ed. D., Acting Associate Dean for Research and Research Professor, Dept. of Counseling and Human Development Services, College of Education, University of Georgia

"The values you have counseled the reader to accept or teach are as refreshing as they are mandatory. They will establish a foundation for our children's growth, individual worth, and role within family, community, and peer culture." -- James W. Mullins, Ed.D., Exec. Director, House of Representatives Research Office, State of Georgia.

"I regret that I did not have this book available in my career as a public health and school nurse. It is simple enough that any teenager can read and understand it.--Rebecca B. Niolon, retired R.N. and grandmother.

ACKNOWLEDGEMENTS

For help received in the development and production of this book, I feel a deep sense of gratitude to many people. To name all of them would be difficult because there were many.

I especially thank Beecher DuVall, Ed. D., a high school counselor, who field tested the manuscript with students and parents, and who wrote the Foreword. His belief in the need and quality of this work kept me going when others sought to discourage me from taking on such a sensitive subject as values education.

A special thanks to my co-author, Sarah Swoszowski, who collaborated, reviewed and rewrote portions. She supplied me with college references that improved my knowledge of motivations and behavior. Her contribution has been considerable.

Also a special thanks to James Mullins, Ed. D., Executive Director of Research for the Georgia General Assembly and his staff. Dr. Mullins was very encouraging and helpful. Two famous people, Dr. C. Everett Koop, and James Michener, the famous writer, also offered encouragement.

Others who edited portions or made valuable suggestions were Terri Weaver, Father Richard Morrow, Wm. Banick, Alexa Selph, my daughter Terri Van House, and Sergeant Debra Roberts of the Gwinnett Co. Police Department.

Others who read the manuscript, offered encouragement, and wrote testimonials include Marie Schivaree, Naida Speed, Carmel Vaughn, Dr. Wm H. Hill, and those whose names appear with the testimonials.

Last, but not least, is my editor, Nancy Badertscher. She cut the text portion to 200 pages without eliminating important matter, while improving readability.

Charles L. "Grandpop" Van House

ABOUT THE AUTHORS

Charles L. Van House, Sr. the principal author, discovered early in life that he was gifted with a special ability to analyze complex subjects, to sort out basic patterns, and to translate them into simple language.

He is retired as a senior officer of a large life insurance company. During his career, he authored the first successful self-study textbook on accounting in life insurance companies, a technical subject. It was used for 16 years in courses sponsored by the Life Office Management Association, an international organization.

During his working years, he became interested in psychology. especially the forces that prompt mentally healthy people to do the things they do. What makes a successful salesman? What gives some people charisma, while others repel? What motivates people to do good or commit crimes?

He was motivated to write this book because he believes the increase in violence between sexes and other crimes are a direct result of deteriortion in standards of personal and family values. He also believes that the trend can be changed only by helping our future citizens develop good values.

* * *

Sarah M. Swoszowski has a M.A. degree in humanistic psychology. This science focuses on behavior of healthy individuals, more specifically on:

(1) *Relationships* between individuals and individuals to society and the world around them;

(2) Potential for behaving intentionally and *accepting responsibility* for actions; and

(3) *Self awareness* and *will to create* meaning, identity, and fulfillment in life.

She is the mother of two young men and is presently studying for a doctorate. She served as collaborator and consultant on this book, making many suggestions and rewriting parts to give an even balance between the male and female perspective.

THIS BOOK IS DEDICATED

To my sweet wife, Susan, and our grandchildren, Rob, Chris, Jon, Mathew, Jennifer, and Hannah.

In the top picture are Rob and Jon Allen with Grandpop. In the bottom picture, from left to right, back row, are Matthew Van House, Chris Nelson, and Rob Allen. In the front row, Grandpop, Jennifer Van House, and Jon Allen. Inset is Hannah Fraher.

Grandpop Van House

CONTENTS

FOREWORD

This book was written for you, teens. It is about really living. It includes suggestions on becoming happy, popular, successful, and avoiding boredom. It is about things and ideas that are extremely important for the "good life."

Like the Army says, "Be all that you can be. Regardless of what your home, your school, your church or other community agency is trying to do for you, *your successes in life are still up to you.*

The authors have attempted to cover every subject that might be of concern to you at this point in your life. They have dealt with sensitive subjects in a very straight-forward way, which I believe you will appreciate. They don't beat around the bush. If you are looking for solutions to some of life's toughest questions and problems, here it is in *TEEN SELF-ESTEEM*

I have used this book with my students (and their parents) and I have found it a useful guide. This is not just a book to read, it is a manual for living. Every subject presented is one of challenge. Your responsibility is to meet the challenge. Ask questions, discuss subjects in the book with your parents, teachers, counselors, church leaders, and especially your friends. By asking questions, you will find answers. These will become your values.

This book was originally titled *With Love From Grandpop.* I liked this title best because the senior author had in mind only to give you information that has proven successful in his life. He has gathered supporting evidence to show that what you do results in what you get. If you don't like what you are getting in your life, you have to change what you are doing.

For parents, teachers and others who are supporting positive growth in teens, this book is an excellent guide, a road map to successful living, a springboard for discussions, and a basis for sound decision-making. Teens must explore the world around them and take from it that which they can most value. This book gives options, is filled with facts, and is based upon many personal successes and some failures.

You have my best wishes as all of you, together, meet life's challenges, climb mountains, and achieve individual successes.

W. Beecher DuVall, Ed.D, P.C.
Public School Counselor

PREFACE

To Young Adults and Their Parents:

This book covers many things I wish I had known when I was in high school and that aren't covered in text books. It also covers information I would have passed on to my children when they were growing up--*if I had had the knowledge and the time.* I am now retired with time to do research, to sort out what is important, and to pass on to others what I have learned.

Life patterns and values established during the early teens determine whether a young person will become a happy, responsible adult or become one whose life will be devoted to self-indulgence, with many problems and upsets.

During this period, young people begin casting off parental restraints and becoming more independent. By nature and because of lack of experience and knowledge, they take many risks adults would not take.

With sufficient knowledge, young people gain self-esteem and confidence to make instant, responsible decisions when parents aren't around to consult. Otherwise they often react to other young people who seem more knowledgeable.

Parents can help their children build a good value system by showing an interest in their progress and encouraging them. To help them understand their children's motivations, there is a consolidated digest of modern parenting concepts in Appendix A.

The book covers the logic behind traditional values and is consistent with teachings of all religions. The presentation is simple and logical for easy reading.

With Love, From Grandpop

Charles L. Van House Sr.

CHAPTER I

Building a Good Life

Self-esteem is being at ease with yourself and what you can accomplish. It is built upon an understanding of natural life forces and knowing how to apply this knowledge to enjoy life while achieving successes.

Happy people spend most of the hours of each day in routine living and following repetitive schedules, but there also is much time for pleasant interaction with other people, for improving skills, and for fun.

HAVING FUN

Happiness can come from a smile, a hug, or a good meal. But, a happy life doesn't just happen. It must be built on a sense of responsibility toward yourself and others.

It is natural for young people to take risks as they seek pleasure and independence. They feel they would never have fun if they worried about all of the problems parents caution them about. They can enjoy the thrills of riding a roller coaster without giving a second thought to all of the precautions the operators took to make the ride safe.

At any age, enjoying life, or more simply being happy, is, as it should be, a primary goal in life. A happy person spreads cheer. Live each day to the fullest, but keep in mind that your future happiness depends upon many of the things you do today.

Let's digress for a minute so Grandpop can tell you about his youth.   This story serves a purpose, as you will see.

At your age, I was very insecure and felt very disadvantaged in comparison with my class-mates.   My parents were very strict and constantly preached that children were to be seen, not heard. At Christmas time, we felt lucky to get a nice warm pair of mittens.   I don't recall my parents ever saying they loved me, or my brothers and sisters, and I don't remember being hugged or kissed.

It was in the heart of the great depression. There were no local jobs available, I had no money to date and Dad wouldn't let me use the old family automobile.

In high school, I scored in the upper ninety-nine percent on standardized tests, similar to the Scholastic Aptitude Tests of today, and wanted very much to go away to college and to get away from my family and the small town of 250 people where I grew up.   Dad didn't have enough income to send me to the University of Nebraska, 60 miles away. Scholarships for first-year college students weren't available in those days, except in very small amounts.

Looking back, I realize my life wasn't so bad, even though I saw it differently then.   Dad was an honorable man and did well raising his family on his low salary.   In fact, he moonlighted at several part-time, responsible jobs, such as secretary-treasurer for the town and as a voluntary fire fighter.   He also did radio repair work from our dining room.

Dad raised a large garden every year with very little help from his grumbling sons.   My mother canned vegetables and fruits all summer, helped raise chickens and baked bread several times a week for her growing brood.   We boys did help with some of the big jobs--such as planting potatoes, picking bugs off the plants and digging up and storing the potatoes in what was called the cave or root cellar for the winter. We took turns running the hand-powered washing machine and clothes wringer every Monday morning before going to school.

There never was a time we didn't have plenty of wholesome food to eat. Meat was doled out sparingly, but we always had plenty of tomatoes, corn, beans, asparagus, cherry pie, and apple pie. We even had ice cream or popped corn on Sunday evenings. We could always fill up on bread and potatoes.

We didn't have television, but, in good weather, there were always enough boys to get together to play baseball or football. In the evenings, we listened to many hilarious comedies on the radio. Week after week, Fibber McGee, on a comedy program, would open his hall closet door and we would split our sides laughing when we heard a loud clatter from falling objects. We never tired of the repetition.

Dad had two sets of books, including many of the classics, that both entertained and educated us. Other boys and some of Dad's friends had novels that we borrowed, such as the Tarzan books and western stories by Zane Grey.

By using imagination and self-discipline, I overcame many obstacles to getting a business-oriented education. I continued to study throughout life and even wrote a text-book for the life insurance industry. When I retired, I was a senior vice president in a life insurance company that was second-largest in Georgia for many years.

In this book, I hope to pass on to you many of the lessons I learned along the way, as well as others learned by research.

This personal story demonstrates that: (1) We seldom appreciate the good things until later, (2) We tend to focus on problems, creating unhappiness, and (3) Obstacles to a happy and successful life can be overcome if we apply imagination and self-discipline.

Most people, including adults, do not realize the important part instincts and emotions play in determining our likes and dislikes, and, as a result, our behavior. We know we like or dislike something, without giving a second thought to what caused these feelings.

The next two chapters will discuss the power instincts and emotions have over actions and will provide some suggestions for developing self-discipline and control over these forces. For now, let's examine more basic information about happiness and how to build a good life.

INGREDIENTS FOR A HAPPY LIFE

If a person is to build a happy life, he or she must focus on and develop skills in many areas. The most important are six that we will call basic ingredients of a happy life.

They are: (1) security, (2) acceptance, (3) friendship, (4) achievement, (5) physical fitness, and (6) consideration for others. There are many others that are interrelated and are covered throughout this book.

Security

The basic ingredient of happiness--over which a teen-ager has little control--is security. This ingredient is provided by parents who offer food, shelter, and love in a family relationship. From this base, a teen-ager can reach out and try new experiences and return to it when he or she tires or is troubled.

Your parents love you and provide security with very little effort on your part. They also try to keep you happy, but this requires some cooperation from you. When you become an adult, security will become more within your control.

Desire for freedom and independence can destroy security. If a person is to be an achiever, he or she must be free to make choices and take some risks. This desire is a natural part of growing up, but becomes less important as a person matures. Young people in love willingly give up freedom for security in relationships. A homeless person will gladly give up his freedom for security.

Acceptance

Acceptance of those things over which we have little or no control is the second ingredient for happiness. This means liking yourself, being proud of your heritage, and making the best of the gifts with which you were endowed on the day you were born.

Few people complain for long about the weather. They may grumble because it is storming, but they soon get over it and go out with the proper rain gear. Of course they are happier when the sun comes out.

Many young people become very unhappy over homework assignments, the fact their parents can't buy them an automobile, the food in the cafeteria, and over other things beyond their control. Somehow they seem to feel that if they make themselves miserable, the people who control these things will do something about them, which is very unlikely.

Infants cry out of hunger, hurt, or the need for attention. They learn that making a fuss gets results. As the infant grows older, the child still retains much of this learned behavior. He may realize his parents can't or won't give him something he wants, but the child won't accept their refusal. He has learned from past experience that if he makes a fuss, it will get him either sympathy or more concrete results.

Mature adults know that making a fuss is the least likely way to accomplish anything. They accept things that are beyond their control. Making a fuss is a strain on the body and it upsets the persons being pressured.

Here's a well-known prayer you might like to memorize and say each morning as you brush your teeth or comb your hair: *"GOD, grant me the serenity to accept the things I can't change, courage to change the things I can and WISDOM to know the difference."*

Friendship

The third ingredient for happiness, which you can control, is friendship. This means not only making friends with many other young people your age, but also getting along well with your teachers, parents, brothers and sisters.

Achievement

A fourth ingredient for happiness is achievement of carefully established goals. Achievement of academic and athletic goals will bring you success in life with many rewards. This kind of happiness results from consistently applied effort.

You will seldom be bored if you plan activities for yourself and others and work to make them successful. Goals should be practical and attainable. Trying to achieve impossible goals is frustrating and will cause you to lose faith in your abilities.

As you achieve goals, you need to set new ones. If you rest on your laurels, life will become boring.

Physical Fitness

The fifth important ingredient for happiness is being physically fit. Those who already have impairments must accept their bodies as they are and get the most out of life in spite of limitations.

We all, including those with impairments, need to keep our bodies in good shape. This requires doing regular strenuous exercises to keep the heart and lungs functioning well, controlling weight, avoiding alcohol and drugs, avoiding venereal diseases and pregnancy, and even brushing teeth and bathing regularly.

Without continual effort, the body will not develop the strength it needs to survive life's stresses. Abuse of the body, in time, will result in loss of energy and will eventually lead to poor health and unhappiness.

Consideration for Others

The sixth ingredient for happiness is consideration for others. Willingness to consider the rights of others, including the rights of parents and teachers, and eventually your mate and children, will have a strong effect on your current and future happiness. Consideration for others also will be important to your success after you finish your schooling.

Various studies indicate that doing something with other people, especially something for them, is the most powerful of all stimuli to health, happiness and longevity. Conversely, ignoring, or being inconsiderate of others' rights, will lead to conflict, which brings unhappiness.

It is not necessary that all of these ingredients be present to be happy. For example, a person with a serious illness can be happy if he or she accepts and appreciates the fact that others are doing all they can to help. A selfish person might feel he or she is happy, but that person would be happier giving time and attention to others.

Note that pleasures, such as hobbies and the love of music, art, sports, and dancing, are not included as basic ingredients of a happy life. Ingredients are input, whereas pleasures are output.

Love of art and good music come from within and can be classed as instinctive reactions. Happiness derived from these instincts can be enhanced by achieving, i.e., studying to gain more appreciation for beautiful things and to develop the skills to create them.

Note also that love and having intimate sexual relationships were not mentioned as ingredients for happiness. Love is happiness provided by security in relationships and consideration for others and so was not mentioned as a separate ingredient. Both love and sex are ingredients of a happy marriage. When combined with a true lifetime commitment, they enhance happiness. Love is the "frosting on the cake" of happiness.

IS HAPPINESS A FREE GIFT?

There is a price to pay for all of the pleasures of life. Sometimes the price is in time and effort expended to accomplish something worthwhile. Many times the price is paid at a later date in feelings of guilt or punishment. Sometimes the price is paid both before and after, as in the case of a person who buys drugs (money before and misery later).

There are few pleasures that are relatively free, such as watching a beautiful sunset, going for a walk with someone you love or watching TV. Happiness cannot be purchased with money. Having a lot of money or other worldly possessions does not automatically bring happiness. Money is a tool that can be used to make us happy--if we have enough of it and use it wisely. But it can cause extreme unhappiness if improperly used or if it becomes a principal goal in life. Billionaires, famous singers and movie stars are wealthy, but their money doesn't buy them happiness.

You are fortunate to be living in a time when science has substantially improved living conditions. You can be cooler in summer because of air conditioning. You can ride about in automobiles and airplanes that are many times faster and more comfortable than the horseback riding and buggies of the early 1900s. You have movies and television to keep you entertained and help you learn. Doctors know more about how to keep people alive and healthy for many more years.

There is a price to pay for all of this progress. Increased knowledge and education are required to manufacture and service all these wonderful machines and to utilize the new scientific information. It forces you to learn how to survive and be happy in a more complex world. This not only forces you to gain more technical knowledge, but also to deal with others more extensively.

Advancements in medicine are resulting in greater and greater population growth. The availability of birth control methods has reduced the population explosion somewhat, but has placed a burden on you to help control it by avoiding unwanted births. This, in turn, forces you to make important decisions about dealing with members of the opposite sex that teen-agers fifty or a hundred years ago didn't have to make.

Years ago, when the only birth control method was abstinence, virginity was a must for all "good girls" and almost a must for young men. Parents, family and community all reinforced this moral code.

Now that birth control methods have been developed, young people may feel pressure from peers to engage in intimate sexual activity. If you yield to the pressure and get careless or you don't fully understand the risks, you may pay the price in the forms of disease, unwanted pregnancy and emotional turmoil.

It will be up to you, and you alone, to build a good life for yourself. Expect some good luck, as well as some bad. Your parents and this book can help you get started in the right direction, but most of the good things you achieve or acquire in life will be the result of setting goals and then applying consistent effort to achieving them.

PRINCIPLES

A successful business manager who was well liked by subordinates and friends was asked on the day he retired, "What is your secret for a happy successful life?"

"I have no secret," he replied. "I have always tried to learn something new every day about myself, about my business, or about dealing with people. When I discovered a sound principle, I wrote it down. Then, I made an effort to apply it to my job and to my life. Soon, it became a part of my behavior. I still make mistakes, but less frequently than before."

Some truths, referred to as "principles," will impress you as being especially important and well worth the time and trouble it takes to memorize them. Therefore, a truth being discussed frequently will be summarized as a principle.* They must be accepted as general truths, not absolute truths. You will find it profitable to think of situations where each principle applies.

Here's the first PRINCIPLE which summarizes the above discussion: *IT IS NOT WHAT YOU LEARN OR SAY BUT WHAT YOU DO THAT COUNTS.* It means learning basic truths so thoroughly they control your actions.

---

* A table of principles to serve as a quick reference guide can be found in Appendix B.

LEARNING FROM PERSONAL EXPERIENCE

It is natural to want to make your own decisions without interference from adults. This is particularly true in matters of love and sex, where instincts and emotions lead people to discount facts learned by personal experience.

The following is a quote from Ann Landers, the advice columnist: "Every day we all must make decisions that determine the direction in which our lives will move. No one, no matter how wise, can make the right decision every time. To err is no disgrace. The disgrace lies in not learning from our mistakes, not picking ourselves up, dusting ourselves off, and trying again."

CHAPTER II

Motivational Forces

Have you ever done something impulsively that turned out badly, and wondered what made you do it?

Values, instincts and emotions motivate people to act. If we understand how these three forces interact and how to use them, we are better able to avoid trouble, to get action out of other people, and to motivate ourselves to achieve good things.

INSTINCTS

The dictionary defines instinct as being an inward unconscious prompting that incites humans and creatures to those actions which are necessary for their guidance, preservation, and development. It also is a natural response to stimuli.

All of us feel that our actions are based on reasoning and the desire to obtain a certain result. On the surface, this is true, but instincts have almost as much effect on our actions as do knowledge and reasoning.

Hard to believe? Consider how instincts and emotions cause some young people to like school and others to dislike it.

First, let's deal with those who like school. Young people instinctively enjoy exploring and doing new things. They like to use imagination and dream dreams of wonderful things. When they study, they find some dull material, but they also find many wonders, puzzles to solve, and thrills in achieving and learning new things.

A desire to be accepted by others and to receive praise and approval also are instinctive. Young people who like school have found that growing in knowledge and winning approval from others satisfies these instinctive desires.

Now for those who dislike school. To rest and sleep are instinctive. We all need a certain amount of relaxation to survive. This includes relaxing by playing and watching television. Some dislike school because it requires effort, which is reacting to the resting instinct.

Others who dislike school have relaxed too much in the past, so that they fell behind in classes. This caused loss of approval by parents and fellow students, and even loss of self-esteem, which is important to everyone. As a result they felt left out of their group, which caused them to dislike school.

In short, the two groups reacted to different instincts, i.e., growing and desire for approval vs resting and loss of approval. Knowledge and judgment (value system) tell us which instincts to follow or ignore.

Other examples: The laborer is motivated to work by a survival instinct. The scientist is motivated by desires to explore, achieve and receive acclaim (instinctive desire for approval). The instinct to survive is secondary for him.

The effect of instincts on actions is greater in the case of small children. Their actions are based almost totally and instinctively on what they want or need.

As individuals mature and gain knowledge, the weight of knowledge on controlling actions becomes greater. However, even the most learned men and women are strongly influenced by desire for sex, love, pride (desire for recognition), and, yes, even jealousy.

There are many instinctive drives that influence our actions and emotions. In this chapter we are primarily concerned with those of (1) survival, (2) reproduction, and (3) nurturing. The latter two are interrelated, but are sufficiently different to be separately classified.

The survival instincts are those that cause us to blink if an object is waved near our eyes. They tell us to eat and drink when we are hungry or thirsty, and they cause a baby to cry when wet or hungry. Survival instincts cause us to like food and appetizing odors. This instinct also causes squirrels to store nuts for winter and people to hoard property. It is the source of selfish behavior.

Reproductive instincts cause us to be attracted to members of the opposite sex. They make kissing and love-making fun. They control our desires to be loved, to have sex, and to bring new life into the world.

The nurturing instincts cause parents to love and protect their children from harm. It causes a woman to want a home in which she can raise a family and causes a man to want to protect his wife and children.

This true story about birds illustrates the importance instincts play in the lives of all creatures. It is told in the first person to better reflect Grandpop's personal involvement.

For several years, a family of barn swallows built nests in the top of my boat shelter on the lake where I live. When I took the boat out, they would take off and fly around in circles, fussing because they felt their homes were in danger. I tolerated them because they are pretty, graceful birds.

On the day this was written, just one nest was still occupied. As I walked out on the dock, the babies from the nest took to the air. Two or three took off without difficulty, but one little fellow hit the water after flying 29 or 30 feet. I was about to get in the boat and come to his rescue when I noticed he was valiantly flapping his wings and making headway for the shore, which was about 60 feet away. I stopped and watched. He rested only once. I thought he was worn out and would probably give up. However, after a ten-second rest, he flapped on.

When he reached the shore, which was two feet straight up from the water, he tried to flap up the bank, but fell back into the water. He tried again, and again he fell into the water. On the third attempt he succeeded and flapped up onto a low bush to dry off.

Naturally I silently cheered and marveled how that little fellow, only a few weeks old, had the sense to keep his "cool" and head for the nearest shore. He had probably never before tried his wings, but he didn't panic and drown. Neither did he squawk for his mother, nor did he give up, even though he must have been exhausted long before he reached shore.

This true story demonstrates the tremendous power of instincts in preserving and perpetuating life. The little bird's survival instinct protected him from panicking and drowning. Since he apparently had never before been out of his nest, his parents couldn't have taught him the acts that allowed him to survive."

EMOTIONS

Emotions excite and frequently motivate a person to action. Examples are love, hate, fear, pride, and anger.

Most emotional reactions are caused by instinct. For example, falling in love or getting angry are more influenced by instincts than by knowledge or intent. Romantic love for a member of the opposite sex is generated by the reproductive instinct, and love of parent for a child is generated by the nurturing instinct. Anger is generated by the survival instinct in that we strive to protect our bodies and well-being from a person who ignores or offends us.

Fear, an emotion caused by the survival instinct, protects our bodies from getting into dangerous situations. If we let fear control us, we might jump off a burning building before help arrived. Most people who drown, do so from fear. It causes them to struggle and inhale water, instead of air. Therefore, instincts can harm as well as protect, unless we use knowledge to make logical decisions.

Although pride is normally considered a good emotion, even it must be controlled. The person who brags about his prowess or his achievements will have fewer friends than the person who is humble about his achievements. "False pride" causes some people to be stubborn and refuse to do what they should.

Selfishness is an instinct that causes us to want to hold on to what we have. Selfishness is good if it causes an adult to maintain a nice home for a family and save money for the proverbial "rainy day," old age or a child's education. Selfishness can lead to greed. stealing and taking advantage of others.

Selfishness may stir up hate, jealousy or the desire for vengeance. These emotions can cause a person to fight to protect his territory or property. If harbored, bitter feelings can destroy peace of mind and do far more harm than good.

Very few people can think logically when they become emotional, regardless of whether these are positive feelings, like love and pride, or negative ones, like anger and jealousy.

A person in love has difficulty believing bad about the object of his or her affections. The lover

refuses to accept facts or to evaluate the relationship realistically. Therefore, a person who feels he
(or she) is in love should let a considerable amount
of time elapse before making any long-term commitments or taking action that could have lasting
effect.

Love is a complex emotion. When love is
combined with good judgment, great happiness can
be the result. When instinctive desires, such as
sexual urges, are interpreted as love and are
allowed to control actions, misery and unhappiness
may be the result. Two chapters of this book are
devoted to the various phases of sexually-related
love and control of sexual urges.

The effect of emotion on judgment is most
evident in a case of anger. The typical angry
person will raise his or her voice and tend to
drown out the person who caused the anger.
Emotions might induce a person to take a swing at
someone who offends him or her. An angry person
will not use good judgment and will not listen to
reason.

An impulsive, emotional response can spoil
friendships, turn love into hate, cause divorces, and
even lead to murder. Avoiding an emotional response takes a great deal of self-control. When
things are calmer, discussion or judgment can be
used to effectively solve the problem or to make
peace.

Here is a principle to remember: *WHEN
EMOTION COMES IN THE DOOR, JUDGMENT GOES OUT
THE WINDOW.*

VALUES

Generally people react similarly in situations
where instincts and emotions are involved, but there
are variations by sex. However, there are many
differences in behavior based on what each person

considers important, or more simply, based on his or her VALUE SYSTEM.

A person's value system consists of many opinions on many subjects and, in particular, those dealing with living. For example it includes his or her opinion on the importance of wealth, education, honesty, good looks, good health, good manners, religion, friendship, love, fidelity, loyalty to country, friends, and family.

A person's value system also includes the degree of importance of each value to him or her, such as: whether one is politically conservative or liberal, whether acquiring money and possessions is more important than honesty, and whether making friends should be for fun, profit, or both.

How do we develop values? They are built on a foundation of instinctive drives and modified by our environment and by years of interacting with other people.

More specifically, our senses of hearing, seeing, feeling and tasting interpret the world around us and form the basis for opinions. Although personal experiences have the greatest effect on forming our opinions, other contributing sources are peers, television, and authority figures, such as our parents and our teachers.

Human beings, with their well-developed brains, have the power to choose the good or the bad, to be loving and giving or self-centered and taking. That power is called "judgment."

People have created a complex world where a responsible value system is necessary for happiness. Without it, reproductive instincts would soon cause the world to become overpopulated and people would starve because the land couldn't produce enough food. Then the survival instinct would cause people to quarrel and destroy each other in wars and to murder to get more food and more territory.

A well-defined healthy value system will guide you in building a good life and in making decisions when someone tries to influence you to do something that could be harmful to you and others.

CONTROLLING ACTIONS AND REACTIONS

Instincts and emotions are good forces. They help us live a good and happy life, but, like fire, they can be destructive.

Instincts and emotions are internally generated—so we have little or no control over them. However, *actions and reactions* induced by instincts and emotions arc subject to total control. For example, we do have the power to choose what to do, to say "Yes" or "No" and to act or not act when faced with temptations. We can't say "No" to wanting to go to a party, but we can say "No" to going when we need to study.

The necessary control is supplied by (1) value systems, (2) self-discipline and (3) self-control. The first of these has already been discussed.

After you have established principles that you feel are honorable and unselfish, you must then develop self-discipline enough to live by those principles. Self-discipline is mind control over instincts, emotions, and body. You have a good chance of having a happy life if you exercise adequate control.

The phrase "self-discipline," describes a *premeditated action* whereas the word "self-control" implies *avoiding an emotional, impulsive, or immediate irresponsible reaction.*

If you make a planned or special effort to accomplish something good, such as exercising regularly or saying "No" to an instinctive urge, it requires self-discipline.

If you control a current emotional response, such as remaining calm when someone offends you, you have used self-control.   If you lose your temper, you haven't exercised self-control.

Impulsive   actions   result   from   emotional reflexes (lack of self-control).   We do something because we want to, without thinking of the consequences or whether it was the logical thing to do. Perhaps   we   wanted   to   assert   our   independence, wanted revenge, or thought we were in love.   We didn't, and didn't want to, think about possible consequences.

Establishing good control over instinctive and emotional reactions can help avoid many problems.

CHAPTER III

Take Charge of Your Life

A leader takes action when common sense indicates action is necessary. He or she doesn't wait for someone else to lead or direct.

Leading requires self-esteem. The first step to building self-esteem is understanding how emotions and instincts affect actions and reactions, which was covered in Chapter Two.

The next step is developing self-discipline and self-control, which helps you control actions and reactions induced by instinctive and emotional urges. This chapter will give you information that should help you gain and strengthen that control.

An important phase in developing self-esteem and self-respect is understanding what creates a feeling of insecurity.

INSECURITY

Most people feel insecurity is a weakness. This is not so. It is caused by the survival instinct that protects us against rushing into unknown fields that might cause us harm. Gaining knowledge and experience erases the insecure feeling.

Everyone feels insecure in a new situation where he or she has limited experience. An actor feels nervous when he first goes on stage, but once he starts speaking his lines and senses his audience's reaction, he becomes more secure and confident. His initial feeling of insecurity was caused by fear of the unknown, or more specifically, lack of experience with that particular audience.

In high school, Grandpop was very insecure for a number of reasons, including those mentioned in Chapter I. His coordination also was poor and his penmanship was barely legible, which resulted in criticism. He overcame these handicaps through self-discipline. He spent hours by himself bouncing balls, skipping rope, and filling page after page with writing exercises.

He became a fair basketball player, although he stood only five foot, six inches, a reasonably good tennis player, a better-than-average swimmer, and a legible writer. He has continued exercising strenuously over the years and follows a regimen recommended by the Royal Canadian Air Force for forty-year olds even though he is almost twice that age. As a result, most people say that he looks at least 15 years younger than his true age.

Self-discipline and good health were important to Grandpop as he sought to enjoy life and succeed in business. Most of the information in this chapter reflects much of that determination and dedication.

A teenager's feeling of insecurity (lack of confidence in self) usually results from (1) inexperience in handling life's problems, (2) criticism from parents and others, and (3) drifting rather than using time efficiently to develop skills.

Inexperience With Life Problems

It is normal for teenagers to feel insecure when dealing with others, particularly the opposite sex. They have been protected in home and school environments and have little occasion to deal with others except in these controlled environments.

Instinct causes boys to be interested in girls, and vice versa, but young teenagers, particularly boys, get tongue-tied and have difficulty saying anything meaningful to girls, even when they very much want to. If a girl, or group of girls, laughs about a boy's awkwardness, he gets even more flustered. To many 13 to 15-year-old boys, girls seem flighty and giggly.

Try to realize that all teenagers, including the girls, are insecure until they have more contact with the opposite sex.—This is all a part of growing up and becoming an adult. As teenagers grow older and the natural attraction between sexes takes over, they gain more experience and become more relaxed.

Insecurity or lack of self-confidence frequently is based on how we think we are perceived by others. Usually we are totally wrong because others seldom see in us the things we worry about the most. As you gain knowledge and skills, both from experience and reading, insecurity will go away.

Here is a principle to remember: *KNOWLEDGE IS POWER.*

Accepting Criticism

Each of us sees ourselves as a definite kind of person. We see many good features, but tend to ignore the unpleasant or unfavorable. We are proud of being strong, pretty, intelligent, honest, kind, etc. This is good and makes us happier.

We get angry with anyone who mentions our unpleasant features, even when they are trying to help. If we are unkind, inconsiderate, or have a correctable physical problem, such as excess weight, we choose to ignore these comments or become defensive. This reaction is part of our survival instinct.

Sometimes, we refuse to recognize faults because we lack confidence in our ability to eliminate them. Lack of confidence is frequently caused by criticism. If we are praised for the things we do correctly or better, we gain confidence and a greater feeling of self-worth.

In training their children, parents frequently use criticism that is hard to take. If we feel we can't please parents and others, we have difficulty making decisions for fear of being criticized again. Parents have emotions and make mistakes just like you and I, so we must accept the fact that they are trying to help and not let it destroy our confidence.

A skilled teacher knows that recognizing progress gives students confidence and facilitates learning, but everyone can't be a skilled teacher. Therefore, accept criticism with an open mind and then determine if it was justified. If so, take steps to eliminate the cause.

If you accept criticism gracefully, you will probably receive less criticism in the future and will find that what you do receive is easier to accept. If the person offers further criticism you feel isn't justified, you can say nicely that you appreciate the interest, but you like things the way they are. Nothing will be gained by quarrelling with someone who is trying to help you. If you respond diplomatically, feelings will be spared and you will feel good about your self-control.

Pride in self and pride in accomplishment makes it easier to accept criticism. Taking charge of your life will give you the strength to ward off many blows to your pride.

Drifting

Non-achievers or drifters are the young people who won't get out of bed in the morning. They wait for Mom to order them to clean their rooms. They put off doing homework until yelled at. They don't participate in extracurricular activities at school. They watch television constantly, monopolize the telephone, and complain that they are bored.

Drifters pick other drifters as friends. When they get into trouble, which is frequently, it is because they drifted and followed these friends instead of doing what common sense (their brains) told them to do.

Too much pleasure wastes a life. Some entertainment and socializing are necessary to develop a well-balanced personality and to relax tensions after a dedicated work effort. Reading is relaxing and develops the brain and communication skills. Personal involvement in sports develops the body and electronic games develop reaction time. However, too much time devoted to pleasures interferes with developing other talents that are needed for future success and happiness.

If you are drifting, you need to recognize what you are doing to your current and future happiness. If you are to have a happy life, you must work to develop self-discipline. Being in control of your life will build your self-esteem.

A philosopher, Leo Rosten, once said:

"Happiness means self-fulfillment and is given to those who use to the fullest whatever talents God or luck or fate bestowed upon them."

DEVELOPING SELF-DISCIPLINE

If you can't do something as well as others, there are many things you can do to gain more confidence. Try to excel in something that will build your pride, but don't stop there. Those who take control of their lives will not feel inferior.

Remember the little prayer we suggested about accepting things we can't change? If you don't worry about things you can't change and work to achieve the good things that are in your power, you will build confidence in yourself.

It is more important to correct deficiencies than it is to develop new skills. Both are important, but once your basic skills are honed, new skills are easier to acquire. If you apply only 15 minutes a day to correct deficiencies that are subject to your control, you will be amazed at how rapidly you build confidence and skills.

Once you get control of your life, it will be easier to do things that are good for you, such as regular exercise, daily studying, and healthy reading. Healthy reading means classics, clean fiction, biographies, news magazines, and non-fiction magazines, such as Readers Digest.

Projects at the end of this chapter will help you develop self-discipline and build confidence. Find one that interests you and excel in that one. As your skill increases so will your self-confidence and self-respect. A system is described for keeping track of progress and embarking on new ones as you find time.

Here's a PRINCIPLE to memorize: *SELF-DISCIPLINE BREEDS SELF-ESTEEM.*

PHYSICAL FITNESS

One of the best ways to develop self-discipline is through exercise. Exercise has a double effect--it develops the body and helps the mind take control of the body. Doctors tell us that the healthier the body, the healthier the mind. Of course some brilliant men and women have weak bodies, and many sports heroes have inferior intellects--but these are exceptions. Professional athletes usually have above average intelligence because more than physical prowess is required to develop top skills.

If you develop only the mind and ignore the body, it stands to reason you will be considered intelligent. Conversely, if you develop only the body, it will be strong and the brain will be less developed. If both the body and brain are exercised, the individual will be more alert, well-balanced, and happier. Physical exercise helps your circulation, makes you feel more alive and increases your desire to be more active. It also helps reduce stress, calms a person and clears the mind.

If you haven't been exercising, your body will resist at first, and it will be difficult to get started. Once you get moving, it becomes easier. As you progress on to more difficult exercises, you will find you are feeling more energetic, more alive and more in charge of your life.

Few teenagers exercise enough. The three most common problems are (1) false Pride, (2) lack of Equipment and, (3) lack of time. Let's look at these to see if they are legitimate.

False Pride

A person who has not been involved in sports or in an exercise program becomes easily discouraged when embarking on a physical fitness program. The reasons vary, but often the person is embarrassed over not being able to perform smoothly or as well as more experienced people.

If you are to take charge of your life and become relaxed in social situations, you must learn to laugh at yourself. Others then will laugh with you and help you become better coordinated.

Many people will be willing to help, provided you ask them, show your appreciation and show a positive attitude. Focus your thoughts on their skills, not your own inabilities.

If you hang your head in a group situation and mumble about not being able to do the exercise, everyone will be reluctant to offend you and will leave you alone to suffer by yourself. So why not swallow your pride and get on with improving your physical and social life?

Being humble and able to laugh at yourself will help you become popular and make friends. It also will help you learn to dance and to participate in other group activities.

Equipment

It is not necessary to buy expensive equipment or to join a club. Exercises requiring little equipment include: (1) situps, pushups, jumping jacks, running in place, and jogging (2) bouncing a basketball, soccer ball or tennis ball rapidly (3) riding a bicycle or peddling a stationery one, (4) skipping rope and (5) fast dancing.

Baseball and basketball players need to learn to handle a ball smoothly. Dancers need to learn rhythm. One of the best ways to train your muscles to react smoothly, rythmically, and precisely in a sports-type situation is skipping rope. As you become more relaxed, try ball bouncing or exercising to music. Music is what makes jazzercise so much fun.

Many of the exercise books on the market relate to fads and special equipment. Swimming develops many muscles at one time but may be expensive because it may require joining a club. Clubs and equipment can help you if you can afford them and haven't developed enough self-discipline to exercise by yourself. Avoid machines that tend to develop special muscles, not the whole body.

Time Schedules

After you get started on a regular schedule, you will feel so much better physically that you will actually accomplish more in other areas, making up the time consumed by exercising. You will be more alert and active well into the day.

One of the best times to exercise is in the morning, even if it means getting up a few minutes earlier. Never exercise just before you go to bed because the heart stimulation can keep you awake. Exercise up to an hour before going to bed, provided you read or study for that last hour to help your body relax. Write down a specific starting and stopping times and honor them.

If you can get a friend to exercise with you at a mutually agreeable time, such as after school, it will help you set schedules and you will have more fun--provided you can resist competing or "showing off." Follow the schedule when your friend isn't available or gives up the program. You are not developing self-discipline if you depend upon a schedule set by someone else.

Developing an Excercise Program

You can develop your own exercise program from the above suggestions, or ask your physical education teacher to help you develop one. There also is a suggested program in Appendix E. If you have a physical disability, consult a physician before doing an exercise that could be a strain on your heart or lungs.

Select four or five different exercises to develop most of your muscles, your lungs and your heart. If you do just one exercise, such as ride a bicycle or walk fast, you may develop your legs, heart, and lungs, but your back and arms will be neglected. Continue for at least five minutes after you are puffing hard; more if you also are trying to lose weight.

In developing a program, be sure it allows for progressing into more difficult exercises as your skill increases. Revise your schedule weekly to increase the pace slightly,

Too many people, regardless of age, try to do too much, get totally exhausted, and never try again. Following a strict progression schedule, which requires self-discipline, allows you to achieve a much higher level of physical fitness within a few months without overdoing.

Here are three principles to remember:

(1)   A   REGULAR   SCHEDULE   AND   SEVERAL DIFFERENT EXERCISES ARE REQUIRED TO DEVELOP AND MAINTAIN A HEALTHY BODY,

(2) YOU GET OUT OF LIFE WHAT YOU PUT INTO IT, and

(3) "A QUITTER NEVER WINS AND A WINNER NEVER QUITS."

This third principle assumes that the task was worth the effort before you started and that no problems occur that might justify delaying completion. For example, if you set out to run a mile and are totally exhausted at the end of a half-mile, stop for today, but run a little farther each day thereafter until you complete a mile run. As long as you keep trying at set times, you haven't quit. You're just behind schedule.

If you have trouble getting started on a project, but keep going once you get started, here's a suggestion that works for most people. When you feel a little lazy or reluctant to get started, try saying this:

"One for the money
Two for the Show
Three to make ready
Four to go."

Then jump up on the word "go."

AVOIDING BOREDOM

Being bored need not be a total loss. It means you have the time to develop skills to improve your life, which will build your self-respect and a happier and more successful future.

Anyone who is mentally and physically active will   seldom   be   bored.   Here's   a   principle   to memorize: *BOREDOM INDICATES AN OPPORTUNITY TO IMPROVE THE QUALITY OF LIFE.*

There are two things that cause boredom; not using enough imagination; and not appreciating what we have.

It is easy to be a drifter and wait for something which may or may not happen. We have to have imagination enough to think of things to do, including things that will help others and things that will develop our personal skills.

Every teenager lives in a slightly different world, so no one solution for appreciating and utilizing available facilities will work for all.

Imagine yourself living on a farm. There are no other young people around, so you have to entertain yourself. Both boys and girls can get interested in growing livestock. It is fun to watch a calf develop into a healthy large animal if you care for it properly, and a dog can be a special friend that goes fishing or wanders the fields and woods with you.

In a small town, there are more opportunities to participate in sports. There is more freedom to do things that interest you: building things, learning how to cook, play the piano or other musical instrument, or just reading. The farm youth would never have fun if he or she waited for it to come from others.

Now imagine yourself in a big city with people all around you. Since friends make for fun situations, you have lots of opportunities for fun. Unfortunately you have more opportunities for getting into trouble, so you must use your imagination to minimize risks. You have some of the same opportunities for self-development that the farm youth has, but you also have access to better libraries and entertainment facilities, museums, parks, etc.

Getting involved with others in board games, cards, or sports is guaranteed to eliminate boredom. This is also a way to make friends. Few people get bored when they interact with friends and family.

There will always be people who have more advantages than you, but there will be many who have fewer advantages and harder lives. Those with the most disadvantages have more time and a greater opportunity to develop self-control and inner strengths.

ACTION SECTION

Before going on to the next chapter, make a list of things (projects) you hate to do, but you know you should do. Use notebook paper so you can keep the list and related papers together in a ring binder for easy reference. At the top of the page. put the title "Plans for Taking Charge of My Life". Then write your name. Hereafter, this will be referred to as your "Take Charge" list.

Taking charge of your own life doesn't imply trying to control others, so don't include such projects. Also don't include getting up in the morning. You already know when you should get out of bed and know it has to be done every day. Once you get started following a good schedule, you'll find it easier to hop out of bed.

Insert how and when you can do each chore or job. When scheduling the projects, pick a particular time each day when you are likely to be free of conflicts. It might be immediately after school, after supper, or an hour before you go to bed.

Add to the list things that you would like to do, but just never seem to get done. Don't include easy things. Doing so defeats your goal of building self-discipline. You want to list things that take planned effort. Starting a specific exercise program should certainly be on the list. Now go through the list and give a priority to each item, using Number 1 for the item that will help your physical well-being the most.

On a separate sheet of paper, write down how you plan to carry out the three projects with the highest priority. If you want to go out for an extracurricular activity at school, be sure to show what you will do during the same times when school is not in session. Vacation time is when you have the most time to improve your skills.

Here are some ideas for your list:

(1) Develop a physical skill, such as swimming, dancing or throwing a baseball, football, or basketball, or learning to play tennis or golf.

(2) If you can carry a tune, perhaps you would like to learn to sing some popular songs or play an instrument. A person who can be a lead singer is always popular at parties. Songs can be easily learned from recordings.

(3) Learn to cook. Both boys and girls enjoy following recipes, turning out something special and being creative. Once you have learned most basic recipes, you may try inventing dishes, but be sure you know what the various ingredients will do. Too much salt will ruin any dish, and too much baking powder will ruin a cake. If you make a cake, you might do it from scratch rather than from a pre-mix. It'll take more skill, be more fun, and will taste better.

(4) Take up a hobby, such as building models, bird watching, or collecting stamps, baseball cards, comic books, matchbox covers, butterflies, etc. Do the daily crossword puzzle in the newspaper to improve your vocabulary. Do jigsaw puzzles to challenge your powers of observation and patience. Jigsaw puzzles can be inexpensive at flea markets and garage sales.

(5) Get involved in community service programs. Most hospitals and nursing homes need volunteer help. Call one near your home and ask a volunteer supervisor what you can do.

Imagine being an elderly person in a wheel chair or in a nursing home with nothing to do except talk to other old people or watch the TV. Wouldn't you be thrilled if two young people came in and said, "Hi, we're the cheer-up team. Would you like to talk to us?"

Some old people complain because they feel neglected. If they do, say something like, "We can't help you with that kind of problem and talk of unpleasant things is so depressing. Can we talk about pleasant memories or the weather?" Most of them will immediately cheer up and cooperate.

A special benefit of volunteering at a nursing home will be a better understanding of the importance of being around people who love you. None of us know what the future holds, but the person who plans a life with a loving mate and well-disciplined, loving children has a much better chance of having loving people around when he or she is old.

(6). Analyze your deficiencies and develop programs to correct them. This could include problems with weight, physical coordination, math, penmanship, and more.

(a) If you are overweight or underweight, write down rules that you intend to follow to lose or gain weight. Of course, you could join an organization such as Weight Watchers to lose weight. It might be difficult without help, but you will improve your self-discipline if you can set and follow a system you worked out.

There are many ways to control weight, including counting calories, reducing portions of starchy, sweet or fattening foods, and increasing portions of fruit and vegetables. Avoid eating between meals. If you are underweight, add exercise and increase proteins.

(b) If you are a slow reader or wish to develop your mental capacity, establish a daily reading schedule. If you want to skip weekends, write that down. Pick easy books and magazines first. Mystery stories are always great for easy concentration. As your reading speed increases, switch to more difficult material. Include some biographies and some science fiction.

(c) If you have difficulty with mathematics, memorize multiplication and division tables, or ask your teacher for suggestions on how to improve your skills. Consider asking your parents for other suggestions. It's time you began to paddle your own canoe, but don't swamp your canoe by failing to call for help when you need it.

(d) If your penmanship is pinched or scrawling, schedule 15 minutes a day to make concentric ovals on ruled paper, trying to keep them between lines. Another exercise is to push-pull a ball point pen between lines, trying to keep the pen-made lines close together without overlapping. A third method is to copy from a book or magazine, trying to make the letters neatly and the bottom of letters fall exactly on a line.

Work on several projects at a time, perhaps one mental and one physical. After you become proficient and in control of one self-discipline project, select another. As you reach a goal for a project, you will thrill with accomplishment. There will be no teacher to grade you, but you will know you did it by yourself and you are gaining control over your life.

Add new projects to your list from time to time. Don't get so wrapped up in one project that you don't have time to take on others. When reading becomes too entertaining, try something else that will challenge you. Even TV will become more interesting during the fewer hours you devote to it. Don't eliminate an item because it takes too much effort.

On long-term projects that can be broken down, make a separate sheet listing the smaller ones. Show the approximate date you will start each phase. In this way, you will be able to show progress, and you will want to continue developing self-discipline. For example, if you decide to learn carpentry or develop a hobby in wood-working, start with simple projects, such as a small box with a lid.   Perhaps, Mother would like one for her recipes.   Then move up to a birdhouse, a toy wood train for brother, etc.   A girl might want to try a simple sewing project or whatever suits her fancy.

Now is the time to begin taking charge of your life. Start making the list NOW.

CHAPTER IV

Love and Related Emotions

Love is a many splendored thing.

Love makes the world go 'round.

Everyone loves a lover.

Love sells diamonds and love creates new life.

Love is wonderful.

Many things can be said about love. If you have it, you don't want to analyze it, just enjoy it. However, if you don't understand what attracted you to an individual, it will be more difficult to build and preserve your love. Understanding instinctive drives will help you keep your love on track.

Enjoying the company of a person of the opposite sex is one of the greatest pleasures in life. Successful marriages are based on the love of two mature people who would enjoy each other's company without sex. When you add sexual relations and a lifetime commitment, living together and raising a family can be a fulfilling experience.

Many people use the word "love" as being interchangeable with sexual attraction--so many people assume they are one and the same. Being "in love" with a member of the opposite sex may be an exhilarating feeling, but, *if* it is sexual attraction rather than true love, this kind of "love" can have more ups and downs than a roller coaster.

This chapter will help you determine the difference between stages of love and the instinctive reproductive drives of males and females.

All of this should: (1) help you plan a better, happier and more permanent love life and (2) put you at ease with your sexuality.

More than half of all marriages end up in divorce. Many couples were in love when they married, but circumstances, false expectations and lack of commitment caused them to grow apart. However, many other couples were not truly in love when they married. To understand this statement, you need only review the various stages of sex-ually-oriented love: (1) puppy love, (2) infatuation or euphoric love, and (3) true love.

PUPPY LOVE

How do people know they are truly in love? Some people say, "If you have to ask, you aren't in love." That is true, but too many people think they are in love when they are just sexually attracted to another person.

The phrase "puppy love" might be defined as the first throes of being attracted to members of the opposite sex. It involves imagination without any particular sexually related *activity* or body contact, such as holding hands or kissing.

Many teenage girls are in love with love. They also imagine themselves to be in love with movie stars and singers. Many boys feel they love a pretty teacher or babysitter. A typical teenage girl also may imagine she is in love with a boy who flatters her and gives her a lot of attention. A boy reacts the same way when a girl notices him and goes out of her way to talk to him. This is puppy love.

INFATUATION

Infatuation is used to describe a strong attraction between a boy and girl that doesn't have the necessary elements of a permanent relationship. The dictionary definition of infatuation is the next principle you may wish to memorize: *INFATUATION IS AN UNREASONING PASSION OR ATTRACTION."*

Note in particular the word "unreasoning." Infatuation is highly emotional. It is the result of a natural INSTINCTIVE attraction between two members of opposite sexes, and usually the result of courting and stirring up of sexually related instincts.

You are strongly attracted to anyone who listens to you, says sweet things, or hugs and kisses. You are happy with the whole world, especially when you think about him or her. A typical teen-ager and many adults interpret this attraction as being love. It might be exciting and euphoric, but it is not love. It is infatuation.

A relationship based solely on sexual attraction usually doesn't last, but can change to true love. Approaching adulthood, you will go through infatuation several times before you really fall in love. The sexual attraction of infatuation may disappear the first time there is a serious difference of opinion or when one partner tries to exercise control over the other.

Infatuation seldom lasts as much as a year. Opposition by parents or others can extend the period, in part, because of a desire for independence and, in part, out of loyalty to the lover. When individuals in a group are persecuted, they band together for sympathy and strength. This is also true in case of a twosome that can't be open about a relationship.

The younger the individuals, the shorter the period of attachment. The reasons vary. One teen may want independence, and the other commitment. These self-centered desires cause quarrels. The couple may go steady for a year or more, but, as time goes on. they are less committed to each other.

A new term, EUPHORIC LOVE, is coming into use to describe intense, sexually-related love. The definition is almost identical to the dictionary definition of infatuation, but adults want a more mature-sounding term to justify having an affair outside marriage. Both terms describe the same unreasoning sexual attraction, but euphoric love most often implies a more intimate relationship.

Euphoric love may last longer than an infatuation because it involves intimate sexual involvement and the thrill of sharing risks. It could result in true love, but that is not likely because true love can survive only in a secure, unselfish, and trusting relationship.

TRUE LOVE

Now let's see how true love differs from infatuation. The phrase "true love" is used here to clarify the fact that there is a difference between true love and sexual attraction.

The definition of true love is a principle you may wish to memorize. *LOVE IS A STRONG FEELING OF AFFECTION. IT IS TRUSTING AND UNSELFISH.* Each person in love is concerned for the well-being of the other.

In the case of love between a man and a woman, true love takes over when each has made a number of concessions to the other over a period of time and each knows the other's wants and desires. This takes time, and an understanding attitude. It involves the brain, as well as the reproductive instincts.

The phrase "made a number of concessions" implies the couple has had a number of differences of opinion, probably arguments or quarrels, about things that were important to one, but not to the other. Either one gave in, or they compromised.

When we say love is unselfish, we mean that love is being kind, considerate, and compassionate toward others. It also means respecting differences and appreciating each other's uniqueness. True love involves more giving and sacrificing than taking. A happy person is a loving person, and a loving person is a giving person.

Love for a member of the opposite sex makes us feel happy in much the same manner as infatuation. Love in a happy marriage is infatuation that has matured into a strong affection and desire to please. The "unreasoning passion" of infatuation has been replaced with a calm affection and recognition of and acceptance of each other's faults and good qualities. Each person develops a feeling of trust and freedom to share confidences with the other in a relaxed atmosphere.

True love is comfortable, like an old shoe or slipper. It is there when you need it and it feels good. If a relationship causes one or the other to be jealous, to worry or to be very unhappy when apart, but exciting when touching, it probably is not true love.

Building and preserving true love can be compared with growing flowers or vegetables. If the plants are properly watered and fertilized, they will bloom and add beauty and comfort to the world. But they require correct and constant care, or they will wither and die. Too much water or fertilizer is as bad as too little.

Remember this principle: *TRUE LOVE CAN EXIST ONLY BETWEEN PEOPLE WHO ARE CONSIDERATE OF EACH OTHER.*

Some couples say they fell in love when they first met. This is unlikely because a person can't feel strong affection for a person he or she has just met. One might like a person's smile or attitude, but that is neither affection nor love. What probably happened was that each liked the looks or personality of the other and tied it to a mental image of a desirable lover.

After getting better acquainted, most love-at-first-sight couples find they have little in common. In truth, the first attraction was a simple reaction to being noticed by a friendly person. This was followed by sexual attraction as they dated each other, hugged, and kissed. Finally, when they have had time to really know each other, their association resulted in true love.

TRUE LOVE IS INTERNAL, NOT EXTERNAL. It can't be turned on at will. It grows from within over a period of attention and affection. For this reason, even a spouse may not receive true love if he or she doesn't earn it by being trusting and considerate. Words do not create love, but actions do.

Each spouse is entitled to sexual relations, a faithful mate and a helpful companion. When one doesn't demonstrate love and insists on his or her marital rights, ignoring those of a mate, he or she may find love and rights disappearing in a divorce. If one becomes selfish or jealous and tries to limit the freedoms of the other, love will die quickly.

Instinctively, parents love their children and want to protect them from harm under all circumstances, but frequently they put their own desires and happiness ahead of love for their children. Children's love for parents is also somewhat selfish because parents mean security to them. Children trust their parents more than they would an outsider and usually feel affection for a person who treats them well.

Aged parents who are completely dependent are entitled to care and love in return for care given to their growing children.

A young adult can earn and keep parental love alive by growing in maturity and accepting responsibility for his or her actions and by being helpful.

Some children, and even teen-agers, will tell you they don't love their brothers or sisters, but they always stand together when one member of the family is attacked by an outsider.

Here is a principle to remember: *MAKING LOVE IS DEMONSTRATING AFFECTION AND GIVING AND SACRIFICING FOR THE OBJECT OF YOUR AFFECTIONS.* It does not necessarily involve body contact, although quick kisses, hugging, and holding hands might be considered truly making love if closeness and thoughtfulness are motives rather than sexual desires.

To clarify, here are analogies on the difference between infatuation and love: Infatuation is like a fire produced by burning paper. It is easy to ignite and the flame burns brightly. However, it burns out quickly unless fed solid fuel. Love, on the other hand, is like a slow steady fire burning more solid fuel. It is difficult to ignite. The red coals aren't as spectacular, but the fire provides steady warmth for a long time. Sex is the draft that makes either fire burn hotter.

RELATIONSHIP OF LOVE TO SEXUAL DRIVE

True love and sexual attraction can co-exist, and usually do, in a happy marriage. This double attraction is appropriately called "romantic love."

Sexual urges satisfied within marriage can build a feeling of mutual love to a peak that is comforting and satisfying. Frequently, sex is said to be the glue that binds a couple together.

The expression "making love," as commonly used, is a misnomer. It is usually used by young people to describe deep-kissing and fondling. Movies depict love as open-mouth kissing and going to bed with a member of the opposite sex. These acts stimulate a viewer's sexual fantasies and can be more aptly described as "building infatuation."

True lovers, not in a position to marry, are more inclined to speak tenderly to each other, to kiss softly and to put their arms around each other.

Here's a principle to remember: *BE A HUGGER, NOT A MUGGER.*

JEALOUSY

Frequently young people, and even adults, are flattered when a boyfriend or girlfriend gets jealous.   They interpret this as a sign of love.   It is actually a sign of insecurity, selfishness and lack of love.   When there is love, there is trust and a willingness to allow a reasonable amount of freedom to be friendly with the opposite sex.

If a child throws a tantrum because another child wants to play with his toys, does it demonstrate love for his toys, or selfishness?   Everyone wants to protect what is his.

A girl or woman who is jealous when another woman pays too much attention to her boyfriend or husband is not demonstrating love for her mate.   A wife, in such a case, is reacting to her nesting or nurturing instinct.   She is protecting her home and her family, which represent security to her.

A man who gets jealous of another man who is nice to his wife is less justified because women are less interested in outside sexual affairs and are far less likely to desert their families.

A principle is: *JEALOUSY IS A MANIFESTATION OF SELFISHNESS, NOT LOVE.*

LOVE AND SEX IN THE MEDIA

Many thousands of books have been written about love, sex and marriage.   No movie or TV drama is considered complete without a love interest, frequently involving steamy sex scenes.

All of the sexual activities we see on TV and in the movies were filmed to arouse and appeal to our sexual instincts and romantic fantasies.   Most of these movies, stories, and books imply the couple will live happily ever after. Unfortunately, that romantic theme is not true to life.

Many viewers accept these activities as models for their own sexual behavior, even though they recognize other scenes involving violence are not to be emulated. They know real-life violence would land the hero in jail. Yet they dream of themselves in similar sexual situations.

Advertisers play up sex because it sells products--so they use it to the hilt. A pretty, scantily clad model will get the attention of a man much quicker than a testimonial from a famous person, a grandfather, or grandmother.

Advertising works on the subconscious and the conscious mind. The most effective ads plant in the subconscious mind the desire for a product. Scenes involving sex and violence, in the same manner, can cause a person to unconsciously mix fantasy with reality.

Sensible people, including politicians, have ruined their careers by getting their sexual fantasies mixed up with the realities of life. Sexual instincts and poor judgment are primarily the cause of these problems.

Many people rent films or go to theaters that show sexually oriented activities and avoid movies filmed for general audiences. After seeing a few hundred sexy movies, we are lulled into the belief that this is not fantasy on the screen, but the way everyone lives and loves. Such movies can dull our sense of right and wrong.

A young woman was raped and almost killed by a gang of boys in New York City's Central Park. When one of the boys was asked why the gang did it, he said, "Because it was fun." Obviously, it wasn't fun for the young lady. His and his friends' sense of right and wrong probably was influenced by the brutality and sex in movies. A notorious serial killer of women admitted that sexy movies excited him and lead him to commit his crimes.

Sister Mary Rose, president of Covenant House, a Catholic organization that helps homeless children of all denominations in several cities, made this observation about sitcoms portraying sex between unmarried teen-agers as normal.

"I wish just once one of these TV producers would take a walk through our crisis shelter. Then, I'd introduce him to kids who don't appear in their 30-minute sitcoms. <u>Real</u> kids in really tough situations. I'd ask him to talk to Lurleen....

"Lurleen is a tiny 13-year-old kid who has a pony tail, a nice smile and something else -- a little baby named Tony. 'He's going to have everything I never had, Sister. Everything.' Lureen is also homeless.

"And there's Melissa. She knocked on our crisis shelter door last week, holding a beautiful baby boy named James in her arms. She's going to live at our mother/child center because she has nowhere else to live. Melissa will turn 17 next week.

"And then there's Wendy. She's a wonderful, wonderful child. Her father left her. Her drug-addicted mother abused her. "I thought having a baby would make things better,' Wendy told me. 'But do you know what, Sister? I love my baby, but I don't know how to care for him. I mean, I need a job. I need money. I'm really scared now.'

"And then there are Joanne, Ginny, Betty and Katrina. And so many others. All very beautiful and well-meaning children, holding children of their own," Sister said.

Perhaps, you feel these girls were stupid not to use birth control. You may be right, but no method of control, except abstinence, is totally safe. Methods of birth control are discussed in the next chapter.

Just because something seems normal after we have seen irresponsible activities many times in movies, or have read about them in fiction, does it make such activities right or proper?   Of course not.   So why should anyone accept sexual activity as depicted in the media as normal?

Here is another principle to remember: *SEX IS NOT A TOY, BUT A GIFT FOR CREATING LIFE AND BUILDING HAPPY MARRIAGES.*

CHAPTER V

AVOIDING HAZARDS OF PREMARITAL SEX

Exploration and finding new things to do are fun and exciting. There is little hazard in most of these activities and they are educational. However, there must be moderation in everything. As long as you are conscious of potential hazards, you can live life to the fullest without ever crossing over into danger areas.

Due to modern development in birth control techniques, there is a tendency to "use" sex for pleasure, even with its many risks.

Getting involved in "all the way" sexual encounters before you are old enough and mature enough for permanent commitment is like playing with dynamite or playing Russian roulette. There's a good chance no harm will result, but there is a chance it will blow you away.

In one sense, dynamite and sexual intercourse have much in common. Both are powerful forces. When properly used they are wonderful tools. Dynamite moves rocks and even small mountains to build roads and dams. Sexual intercourse within marriage builds happy, well-rounded lives for adults and children in a family.

When not properly used, both dynamite and sexual intercourse can destroy. Dynamite can destroy the work of many men and even the handler. The consequences of premarital sex are possible mental and physical harm to both participants and even in destruction of an unborn child, with a risk to the woman through abortion.

The major hazards for teenagers who get sexually involved are: (1) Unwanted pregnancy: (2) AIDS or other venereal disease and (3) The loss of freedom before you are ready. These will be discussed in the next three sections of this chapter under the titles: "Unwanted Pregnancy," "Safe Sex?", and "Going Steady."

UNWANTED PREGNANCY

Satisfying sexual urges is essential only to the continuance of the human race. It takes about 20 years to raise a human to adulthood. Doesn't it make sense to control sexual activity until you can support the resulting child? It doesn't take love to make a baby. It just takes two people of opposite sexes reacting to sexual urges.

Recent statistics from the U.S. Census Bureau indicate that more than 40% of first births are conceived outside of marriage. This would seem to indicate that most methods of birth control are not very effective, especially those used by unmarried lovers.

Recently, a Chicago Tribune writer reported that 8% of all women in the U.S. Navy were pregnant at any given time. Forty-one percent of these were single. The article said about half of the pregnancies were not planned. Navy women have access to all types of birth control information, devices and medical assistance. If they can't prevent pregnancy, what chance does a sexually active teenager have?

Next to abstinence, pills are the most reliable means for preventing conception. However, they must be prescribed by a doctor and taken daily, which is hard for a teen-ager to remember. They don't protect against disease and have side effects that can impair health.

The flesh is weak and reproductive instincts are strong. Therefore, if a girl feels she might get so passionate she can't stop short of intercourse, *it is wise to have a fresh latex condom available.*

Partial protection is better than none. Don't tell the boy about it because he may interpret it as an invitation. Don't depend on him to have one or to use it if he does. The only complete protection is provided by staying out of such situations.

Intrauterine devices (IUDs) and diaphragms are devices that must be inserted in the vagina or uterus by a physician. They must also be fitted by doctors, and a gel or contraceptive foam used. They are less than 100% effective, do not prevent venereal disease, and can cause other disease.

Girls frequently believe they can't get pregnant before they begin menstruating. This is not so. If a girl is sexually active, she can become pregnant.

One girl wrote an advice columnist asking whether she could get pregnant if she kept her panties on. The answer is: Yes, if sperm gets on the panties, it can go through cloth and into the vagina.

Some married couples use the natural planning method, also known as the rhythm method of birth control. It is based on avoiding sex each month when the woman is most likely to become pregnant. It requires the cooperation of both parties and some planning, so it wouldn't be reliable for "one-night stands".

In the January 3, 1992 Morbidity and Mortality Weekly Report of the federal Center for Disease Control, it was reported that more than half, (54.2)%, of students in grades 9-12 had sexual intercourse in the past. Of these, 39.4% had intercourse during the three months before the survey. Of those reporting having intercourse, 77% reported using a contraceptive and 45% reported using condoms.

SAFE SEX

The only absolutely safe sex for an unmarried person is abstinence. The natural law, which also is reflected by civil and church law, is that sex urges should be relieved only within marriage after two people have made lifelong commitments to each other.

Youths who are sexually active today usually continue until they marry or contract a serious venereal disease. Most say they use condoms to protect themselves? Just how safe are condoms?

If condoms reduce the possibility of getting pregnant by 85% and getting AIDS virus by 50%, is that safe enough? The following are quotes are from Sept. 1990 *Population Report* of the Population Information Program of John Hopkins University and U.S. Agency for International Development.

With reference to birth prevention, the report said, "Condoms can be very effective. Most studies, however, find that couples relying on condoms are, on average, not as successful at preventing unwanted pregnancy as users of most other family planning methods.

"Typical pregnancy rates among condom users are 10 to 15 pregnancies per 100 women in the first year of use." This is higher than for most other methods of control. "An analysis of major developed-country studies revealed that the first-year pregnancy rate among condom users was 12 per 100 compared with three for oral contraceptives (pills), six for IUD's, and less than one for voluntary sterilization, but twenty-one for spermicides."

The report showed that: (1) unmarried women ages 20-24 in 1982 had 23 pregnancies per hundred women during the first year they used condoms; (2) the rate dropped to 11 per 100 for unmarried women 25-34; and (3) rates were lower for older married people and those unmarried persons with infrequent coital activity (intercourse). It said,

"The lowest rate of 4.2 pregnancies per 100 women in the first year of use was seen in a study of married British clients of family planning clinics."

With reference to disease prevention, the report said, "A substantial number of people relying on condoms to avoid Sexually Transmitted Diseases (STDs) contract them nonetheless.

"Ten studies of HIV transmission found a risk less than half that for nonusers. An analysis for the World Health Organization (WHO) found that condom users faced a risk about two-thirds that of nonusers of developing gonorrhea, trichomoniasis, or chlamydial infection. Condoms offer less protection against STDs, such as herpes simplex, that can cause lesions in places not covered by condoms.

"In a 1982 study, women relying on condoms faced a risk of pelvic inflammatory disease that was 40% of the risk faced by other women. Similarly, a recent study found that, when women's sexual partners had used condoms for at least one year, their risk of having an ectopic (abnormal) pregnancy was 75% of the risk faced by women using other or no contraceptive method. In a recent study at least one year of condom use cut the risk of cervical cancer in half."

The report said, "Laboratory studies prove that sperm and disease-causing organisms cannot pass through intact latex condoms. They normally contain no holes, even of microscopic size. Laboratory tests show that STD-causing organisms cannot penetrate an intact latex condom. This includes HIV, which causes AIDS.'

So, why don't condoms provide better protection? The report said, "Incorrect use may explain some pregnancies and infections among condom users. Mistakes that may cause tears or breaks include: snagging the condom with fingernails or rings, reusing condoms, unprotected contact while starting or ending intercourse, and allowing the condom to slip off and spill semen.

"Little is known about how sexual behavior and skill affect breakage. Studies have reported breakage rates ranging from less than 1 to 12 per 100 during vaginal intercourse." Two U, S. studies showed 7% breakage. One, a North Carolina study, showed half of the breakage occurred before or after sex. In another study, men broke condoms more often with girlfriends than with their wives.

"Other studies showed that a preference for 'dry sex' (no artificial lubricant) may contribute to breakage. Mineral and vegetable oils substantially weaken latex in five minutes or less. These oils are found in common products such as petroleum jelly, skin lotion, and cooking oil. Products that contain water instead of oil—for example, glycerin, egg white, and K-Y jell—do not damage latex. Neither does spermicidal jelly or foam.

"Exposure to ultraviolet light, heat, humidity, and ozone makes latex deteriorate and weakens condoms. The longer exposed to these conditions, the more easily they break."

In summary, we can conclude that (1) condoms do offer some protection for those whose hormones and instincts are out of control, (2) the danger of becoming pregnant or contracting STDs for sexually active young people is very high with or without condoms, and (3) *there is no "safe" sex.*

Some venereal diseases are painful but can be cured. Others, such as Herpes Simplex II, can only be treated, and can reappear and limit sexual pleasure forever after.

If you have engaged in sexual intercourse, it is important that you be aware of symptoms of venereal diseases and seek medical help immediately if you have sores or pimples in the area of the sex organs, burning or itching of the penis or vagina, and abnormal discharges when urinating, accompanied by a low-grade fever. Syphilis sores may appear on the lips, tongue, tonsils and sex organs.

Symptoms of the more serious diseases, such as syphilis and AIDS, do not appear until months or even years after intercourse. Therefore, the infected person may not be aware that he or she is spreading the disease. Even though he or she is aware of being infected, few will tell the proposed partner even when asked. A person who has been having sex is strongly motivated to continue.

C. Everett Koop, who was U.S. Surgeon General for many years, had this to say about AIDS. "When you have sex with someone, you are having sex with everyone they have had sex with for the last ten years, and everyone they and their partners have had sex with for the last ten years."

You can obtain more information on diseases from advice booklets by Abigail Van Buren and Ann Landers (Dear Abby and Dear Ann). The address for ordering the pamphlets as well as hotline numbers are included in Appendix D. Other sources are local health departments and the Red Cross.

Here's a story of the sexcapades of Gladys, who became sexually active at 15 with her steady, Bob. Her mother came home early from work one day and caught them in the act. Rather than risk having a pregnant daughter, she took Gladys to the family physician and got her a prescription for birth control pills.

Gladys' flirting eventually led to her break-up with Bob. On the pill, she felt free to have sex with any boy who showed her a good time and she started on a free-wheeling sex life.

Bouts with gonorrhea and genital warts made her cautious for a few months and damaged her reputation after two boys contracted gonorrhea after sex with her. Soon, however, she was back in full swing and giving of herself freely to attract boys.

She finished high school without other serious consequence and went on to college. Her reputation followed her, and she had no trouble getting dates. With the sex came dates with men who drank heavily and who made Gladys conclude all boys were sex fiends. She occasionally fought depression and longed for a guy who would respect her.

She contracted gonorrhea one more time. She was cured quickly, but, shortly thereafter, contracted Herpes Simplex II. She took medication to control the herpes, but suffered a flare-up each quarter when the stress of exams approached.

In her senior year, Gladys finally found a fellow she enjoyed being with and fell in love with him. She knew the herpes was contagious only when the herpes sores were present, so she abstained from intercourse whenever the sores reoccurred. He noticed this, but assumed it was caused by moods. When he proposed, she was in seventh heaven, but she knew she had to tell him about the herpes before they married and hoped it would not make a difference.

Unfortunately, he didn't understand. He asked questions about her past. She answered truthfully to be fair to him and, probably, because he would find out sooner or later. He concluded he didn't want a part-time wife and did not believe she could be faithful. They had a violent argument, and she threw the ring at him.

A few years later, after Gladys finished college, she married a co-worker. He wasn't the glamorous, sexy type she had dated, but he went along with her "moods." They both drank a lot, and he also had his moods.

Eventually, she became pregnant. The baby had to be delivered by Cesarean section. Otherwise, the child would have been infected, in which case it probably wouldn't have survived. Neither she nor the baby had further physical difficulties, except for an occasional return of the herpes.

She was lucky she didn't get AIDS or syphilis from her many sexual partners. She didn't get

AIDS because her free-wheeling sex life was before AIDS became so widespread.

Gladys was popular with the boys for six years, but she paid a high price. She had some bouts with sex-related ailments and an alcoholic tendency. She lost the man she really loved, spent a lifetime with herpes and a less desirable mate than she might, otherwise, have married.

Can sexual gratification be worth all of the trouble and risk? As far as the girl is concerned, the answer is a positive, "NO." Even the boy is taking considerable risk. He can walk off if pregnancy develops, but he can't avoid the physical hazards and can be held liable for child support.

GOING STEADY

Parents usually oppose steady dating because they know, from personal experience, that steady dating will put pressure on young people to have sex. After a certain amount of "making out," the natural reproductive urges take over, and the girl gives in even though she knows she is taking a chance .

Here is a story of a typical teenage sexual encounter:

John is 16 and Mary 15 years old. Until recently, Mary's mother did not permit Mary to date boys unless accompanied by another couple. John has just gotten a driver's license and his Dad has been letting him drive the family car on dates with Mary. Both have learned about reproduction in school classes, but neither is fully aware of the psychological and emotional aspects of a close sexual encounter.

The two have fun doing things together, but they have started parking and "making out." Mary enjoys the hugging and kissing and has started letting John put his hands on the more intimate parts of her body. It feels good to her, but she doesn't want to go all the way, even with a condom. She can't understand why John gets so angry when she stops him and she is afraid she will lose him unless she gives in. What went wrong with the relationship?

When a couple gets sexually aroused, which is natural when they get involved in heavy kissing or "making out," it is difficult for them to stop. It is like getting on a slide. The further you go, the faster the ride--so much so that it is next to impossible to stop. John feels frustrated and is taking it out on Mary. They are rapidly approaching a breakup because neither is ready for marriage.

What should they have done? They both enjoyed doing the same things and enjoyed each other's company. They would have been much happier, and it would have worked out if they had continued to be pals and confined their lovemaking to kisses and hugs just before getting out of the car. Neither one should get up tight or feel rejected. They are too young for going steady and should have freedom to date other friends of the opposite sex.

To avoid going steady, you have to develop self-discipline enough to go against the more or less standard practices in your school. If you have many friends of the opposite sex, you will find it much easier to avoid becoming too intimately involved with one person. Also, if you date the less popular, but pleasant boys or girls, you'll find it much easier to retain your freedom.

Let's go back to John and Mary. They both realized they were too young to marry, but felt they were in love. They decided to continue going steady and to abstain from getting so deeply involved. One night they went to a party and had a grand time. Someone spiked the punch without their knowledge, and they felt good. When they got near Mary's house, they parked.

They were both tired from dancing and Mary laid her head on John's shoulder. They talked and laughed and started deep kissing and intense lovemaking.

Mary suddenly realized they were going too far and tried to stop. Her brain was saying, "NO, NO," but her body was saying, "YES, YES". John was so worked up that he was partially undressed and kept pressing. Neither of them had a condom because they had decided not to get this involved. John kept telling Mary he loved her and would marry her if she got pregnant. Finally she gave in. There was sperm all over the car seat and on Mary's legs. He wiped it up with his shorts as best he could and took Mary home.

For several weeks, Mary worried about being pregnant until she finally menstruated. She breathed a sigh of relief because this was a sure sign that she was not pregnant. She called John immediately. He was relieved and happy to know he wasn't obligated to get married. He assured Mary of his love and resolved never again to be caught without a condom.

A few weeks later, they got into a similar situation. This time, John had a condom, but it was slippery and came off. Somehow, sperm got into Mary's vagina and this time she became pregnant. John urged her to have an abortion, but she couldn't bring herself to take the life of an unborn child. He agreed to quit school and get married.

They lived with John's parents for a while until he found a job as an apprentice brick layer. John's mother blamed Mary for ruining John's career and was very unpleasant to her. John's father helped them find a small apartment and paid the rent for a few months until they could furnish it with used furniture.

John was a responsible young man and a hard worker. He did fairly well in his job. By the time the baby was born, he was earning enough so they could pay their own way, except for doctor bills for her and the baby. After the baby was born, Mary loved it, but it had colic and cried a lot.

Mary went to pieces every time the baby cried. Being short of money, she didn't go to the doctor when she should have and lost weight. She smoked constantly.

She also felt betrayed and cheated because she was tied down by the baby, while her friends were still having fun. She complained constantly to John. For a while, he sympathized with her and told her how much he loved her to calm her down. Eventually, he had all he could take, and began drinking beer with his "buddies" every night before coming home. The stress, induced by the alcohol, and her complaining, made him even less tolerant than before.

We'll end the story there, but you know that their problems continued to get worse. However, let's speculate about possibilities. The most obvious is that their marriage will end in divorce.

There is also the possibility of a battered wife and maybe even an abused child. Whenever you have a drinking husband and a complaining wife, violence is a strong possibility. She doesn't have enough education to find a satisfactory job, and she has a child who needs her, so she wouldn't be likely to leave John without someone from outside the family circle taking a hand in the matter.

Since her father came to her rescue in the early days of the marriage, he probably will again. It would be a case of family love helping in time of need. You will be reminded several times in this book how important family can be in times of stress.

Another possibility is, that after a divorce, John could go to jail for non-support of the child or non-payment of alimony. A low income isn't enough to support a family, let alone two people, one with a baby, living in separate households. The financial burden also would prevent John from re-marrying unless he found a wife who could and would help him with the burden.

WHAT A PRICE TO PAY FOR A FEW MINUTES OF SEXUAL INDULGENCE.

Perhaps, you would have solved the problem differently. If Mary had released John and continued her schooling, or had gone to a home for unwed mothers, she could have put the baby up for adoption and gone on with her life.

The child would have been happier because it would be adopted by parents who would give it the love a child needs, not in a home of quarreling parents. Mary would have been wiser and could have gone on to finish her education, even though a year late. When she married, she wouldn't have a mother-in-law who looked down on her as a "tramp."

Another solution would have been to have an abortion. There are both physical and emotional risks involved. These are discussed in the next chapter.

Still another solution would be for Mary to release John and try to raise the baby herself. Here's what happened to Sally who did just that. While she was pregnant, her parents let her live at home and used their health insurance to pay the doctor and hospital bills. This was possible because Sally was still a dependent child.

Sally was a responsible girl and wanted to complete her education. Otherwise, she would never be able to earn enough money to support the child. She also took a part-time job to help pay for her and the child's support.

Sally had to rise in the morning at 5:30 to prepare the baby's bottles, get ready for school, and take the baby to a day-care center. Her mother worked during the day but cared for the baby while Sally worked in the early evening and studied for several hours.

Sally's sleep was frequently interrupted by the baby waking up and needing attention. If Sally hadn't been an unusually mature young lady for her age, she wouldn't have been able to hold up under the short nights and the money and time pressures. Maybe you can figure out how she would handle unexpected illness and getting the baby to the doctor.

By keeping the baby, she put an unfair burden on her mother and brought her "love life" to a screeching halt for a few years. If she had put the baby up for adoption, she would have given a married couple a much wanted child and been freed from from a big responsibility.

That brings us to two principles for memorizing:

TEEN-AGERS ARE NOT MATURE ENOUGH TO HANDLE THE EMOTIONAL ASPECTS AND CONSEQUENCES OF INTIMATE SEXUAL RELATIONSHIPS;

"YOU PAY THE PENALTY FOR A WRONG CHOICE WHETHER YOU MADE IT FREELY OR WERE INFLUENCED BY SOMEONE ELSE."

In the case of premarital sex, this last one is especially important for the girl.

CHAPTER VI

Healthy Boy–Girl Relationships

Every boy and every girl is looking for the perfect girlfriend or boyfriend, but each should realize that (1) he or she isn't perfect and (2) the person being courted isn't perfect either and may have expectations that are selfish or unrealistic.

Eventually each finds the person he or she feels is the most wonderful and attractive. They then quickly fall in love and make commitments that, hopefully, will last for a lifetime of mutual support and happiness.

The close relationships that develop during dating and from associations with the opposite sex stir up instinctive sexual feelings that may be thrilling and euphoric at the time, but can have serious consequences if not handled in a responsible manner. In real life, relationships are seldom as wonderful and romantic as those depicted in books, movies, and TV programs.

This chapter proposes to: (1) Improve your understanding of reproductive drives in you and members of the opposite sex; and (2) Suggest ways to enjoy the company of the opposite sex while avoiding major problems.

Perhaps you are wondering what a grandfather can tell you about relationships that you don't already know. You believe older people don't understand the pressures young people are under to conform to the lifestyles of their friends. Life and loving are different now.

However, when your grandparents were young, they had the same degree of sex drive you have now, the same desires to have a good time, and the same desires for true love. They have an advantage young people don't have—years of experience. They have made mistakes and, over the years, have seen many young people in serious trouble or in unhappy marriages. Hindsight is better than foresight, so why not profit from their experiences?

Sexual urges lessen over the years, but sexual attraction is still there. I still get a thrill when a lady, regardless of age, gives me a hug or smiles at me. One of my fondest memories is an episode that occurred in Athens, Greece, several years ago when my wife and I were touring.

We visited an ancient theater in a rural area. Most of the columns and seating areas were in good condition, but the carvings and statues had been removed to a separate museum. I was so intrigued by the quantity and quality of the craftsmanship that I fell behind the main group.

I suddenly realized it was time for the bus to leave, so I hurried up the steps to the door just as a group of teen-agers entered. One young lady, noticing this nice, old fellow sprinting up the steps, stepped aside, smiled, and patted me on the back. She said something in Greek, which I couldn't understand, but it made my day.

How you apply the knowledge in this chapter is up to you. *IT IS YOUR LIFE. YOU MUST MAKE YOUR OWN CHOICES AND ENJOY OR SUFFER THE CONSEQUENCES OF GOOD AND BAD DECISIONS.*

INSTINCTIVE GENDER DIFFERENCES

Since each person is an unique mixture of personality traits, as well as physical characteristics, this section must be accepted as stating general, not absolute, truths.

Society's *expectation* since the days of cave-
men has been that males would lead and protect,
while females would be submissive and caretakers in
family and many other relationships. This expectation results from the facts that men's bodies are
usually physically larger and stronger, and women's
bodies and instincts are designed for child-bearing.

Male strength is no longer a major factor in
the contemporary world with men engaged in less
physical occupations. Many women are now pro-
viders and are becoming more aggressive, while
many men are getting more involved in caring roles.

Many people contend that gender differences
in personality and behavior are more the result of
learned and stereotypical behavior than instinctive
drives. In this sense, the word "stereotype" means
"a standardized concept that may or may not be
justified by facts."

There is considerable evidence that there are
instinctive differences that are enhanced by learned
facts or "conditioning." These differences are most
apparent in the reproductive and nurturing instincts. Instincts don't change, but traditions and
expectations can change as circumstances change.

Both men and women want love and affection,
and both react to reproductive and nurturing
instincts. Since women's bodies were assigned the
role of bearing children, it is logical to assume their
nurturing instincts, which include love and caring
for others, also are stronger.

To test gender behavior differences in teen-
agers for a later chapter, Grandpop asked forty
teenagers forty-five questions. The following three
showed significant gender differences. Information
in parentheses is inserted here for your
information.

	Boys		Girls	
	Yes	No	Yes	No
Do you like to watch sports on TV? (aggression and desire to win.)	16	5	9	10
Do you like to read romances? (Love and nurturing.)	1	20	14	5
Do you like talking to small children? (Nurturing)	16	5	19	0

Another way to perceive gender differences is to observe the type of magazines, advertising, and television that attracts each sex. The following are some of the principal attractions, but certainly not all.

Males want adventure and science fiction (risk taking), sports (aggression, winning, and competition) and pictures of naked or near naked girls and pornographic books and magazines (reproductive instinct).

Females want fashion and cosmetics (to be attractive to both men and women), romantic stories where the prince wins the hand of the fair maiden (love) and knowledge about sex subjects and attracting men (reproductive instincts).

Fewer women are interested in sports and adventure stories, but many enjoy participating in and enjoying sports contests and building physical fitness.

Few men are interested in fashions, soap operas, and romantic fiction. Both men and women are interested in sexy stories and activity. But how many women look at pictures of naked or near naked men?

All of these are, more or less, harmless reactions to sexual instincts. To prevent a male from looking at females is as difficult as preventing a female from wanting to coo to babies or read romantic novels.

Pornography, including most of the modern films, and sexual drive cause some men and boys to think of women as sex objects rather than warm friendly human beings. Therefore, men should accept such pictures as fantasy, and not true to life.

Many surveys have been made by psychologists to determine how instincts affect our behavior. One psychology textbook* says, "The evidence seems clear that males behave more aggressively than females, particularly when we consider physical aggression." Another survey, cited in the textbook, concluded that a husband's interest in sexual intimacy is greater than his wife's at every age. It is logical to assume this also applies to single young men.

A 1984 survey of college students, reported by psychologist Janet S. Hyde,** asked the question: "How do you feel about one-night stands?" Ninety-one percent of the women said they would feel guilty or anxious, whereas, 50% of the men said they would feel comfortable, relaxed or satisfied.

The survey confirmed the stereotypes that men are more interested in the physical aspects of sex and have a "love-'em-and-leave-'em attitude." Women are more interested, the study concluded, in love and romance rather than the physical aspect of the relationship.

Why this discussion on gender differences?

*Morris, C. G. (1988). *Psychology: An Introduction* (6th Ed.). Englewood Cliffs, N.J.: Prentice Hall.

**Hyde, J. S. (1985). *Half The Human Experience: The Psychology of Women* (3rd Ed.). Lexington, Mass., D. C. Heath & Co.

This knowledge can be used to attract members of the opposite sex, to build healthy relationships, and to avoid problems.

Mutual support builds good relationships. Many good relationships are destroyed when one partner insists on his or her "rights" without giving support and love.

MALE SEXUALITY

As boys physically mature and their voices deepen, their sex urges grow stronger. Male hormones cause them to become more aggressive, competitive, bigger and stronger to protect their future mates. Males also want freedom to experiment without long-term commitments.

Young boys often have an erection when they are just day dreaming and are not even close to a girl. This stirring of sex urges induces a boy to try to score and find a girl who will listen to how he "loves" and "needs" her.

No one really falls in love so quickly. Once a boy has scored, he usually loses respect for the girl. The mystery is gone, and he is not ready for an intimate continuing relationship.

When teen-age boys get together, one of the most popular subjects is sex. It usually takes precedence over sports, school, weather, etc. They frequently tell stories about their sex escapades-- some true, but most fantasies. This is normal behavior growing out of a boy's competitive drive and growing sexual urges.

Boys who brag about how many times they have scored usually don't name names for two reasons. They probably didn't score, but are trying to appear macho. If one did have sex and brags about it, he runs the risk of his name being mud with the girl and her friends.

Most men and boys conceal their emotions because that is what parents and society encourage. They consider tears and any other emotion signs of weakness. Women usually must encourage nurturing activity in males to overcome this stereotypical masculine behavior.

Many men would never marry if they could have all the sex they wanted without getting married. Now that more and more women are agreeable to living with men without marriage, more men are avoiding marriage and responsibility. Fortunately for future generations, most men eventually fall in love and make a lifetime commitment.

The principle here is: *BOYS ARE NATURALLY AGGRESSIVE AND STRONGLY MOTIVATED TOWARD SEXUAL INDULGENCE.*

FEMALE SEXUALITY

When girls get together, they talk about boys, clothes, and social aspects of life. They also may talk about sex but they instinctively are more private about such things, except with very close friends. By nature, they have a stronger desire for warm, close and peaceful relationships than males.

They also have sexual fantasies. Sometimes, a girl is so desirous of being loved, she equates having sex with love and may encourage a boy to "go all the way." However, most prefer to wait until they feel they have a more permanent love relationship.

As girls grow older, their behavior changes to reflect their experiences and their needs. Some will be loving and considerate, while others will become reserved and cautious or hard and unsympathetic. In a relaxed secure environment, most will return to instinctive behavior.

That brings us to a principle to memorize: *GIRLS ARE MORE LOVING AND DESIROUS OF CLOSE RELATIONSHIPS THAN BOYS.*

MALE ASPECTS OF BUILDING GOOD RELATIONSHIPS

A responsible young man who truly loves a girl, but can't support her, will not risk getting her pregnant. He will be concerned about her health and reputation, as well as his responsibility to her.

Abstaining from intimate sex may make you feel like a freak when others are constantly "on the make." What do you care what others think? If you abstain, your life will be less complicated and happier when you find the woman you want to marry.

If you feel insecure around girls, the chapter on making friends will help you. Here are suggestions that apply especially to relationships with girls:

Be nice

Think of girls as being instinctively warm and friendly. Observe how girls treat other girls and treat them the same way. The more effort you expend to make yourself attractive, the more likely they will be attracted to you.

If a girl smiles at you and is nice to you, it means only that she wants to be friendly. Even if you aren't particularly attracted to her, it doesn't cost anything to be nice. Later, you may find she has a hidden beauty that you didn't sense at first. Beauty *is* more than skin deep. Personality can override physical attraction.

Girls appreciate compliments on their appearance and clothes. Compliment them freely-- but don't overdo it. If flattery isn't sincere, girls will sense it and shy away.

The girls you know will some day demonstrate all the loving and caring nature of most mothers. It is probably hard for you to visualize them changing that much--provided they don't lose their faith and trust in men. Women usually enjoy sex under conditions acceptable to them. Normally, this involves a loving, trusting relationship, such as is found in marriage.

When a young man truly falls in love and is ready to marry, he will want a girl who will be faithful and who has had a minimum of other intimate relationships. In all fairness, he should avoid intimate relationships himself.

The nicer boys have more considerate and better-mannered girlfriends. Some girls expect macho behavior from boys, but most will not tolerate sexual remarks. In the adult world, such remarks are considered sexual harassment, subject to legal penalties.

If a girl propositions you and you are not interested, reject the proposition as politely as possible. She may want affection and love so strongly that she thinks being sexually active is the answer. Movies, books, and TV encourage this kind of faulty thinking.

Some girls may want to escape a bad home environment and look at pregnancy as a way out. Would you be willing to marry a girl you really didn't love, to quit school, and to go to work to support a family? What about your future? Could you pay for an abortion if she were willing? What would your parents say?

Don't Dominate

Girls want boyfriends who are sure of themselves and dependable, but not so strong-willed they feel controlled. In this modern day, more wives work outside the home and have the most important role in the family relationship.

Women want to be treated as equals, but also as ladies--with consideration and chivalry. If you think treating girls nice isn't masculine, you'll miss some fun times. A girl will let you know, usually in subtle ways, if she wants different treatment.

FEMALE ASPECTS OF BUILDING GOOD RELATIONSHIPS

When a typical male is ready to marry, he wants to marry a virgin even though he isn't one himself. According to statistics, most men and women have had sexual relations by this time, so male expectations would seem to be unreasonable. If you can avoid sexual relationships until you marry, you will avoid many problems.

Traditionally and instinctively, women want a male who is strong in mind, body, and spirit to love and protect her and her children for a lifetime.

Attracting and Influencing Males

In the next chapter on making friends, there are some thoughts on being attractive to others. Here, we deal more directly with boy-girl relationships.

Most girls and women are only vaguely aware of their power to influence actions of boys and men by using natural sexual attraction and male ego. By making a man feel important to her and encouraging and supporting him when he is down, a woman can stir a man to win games, work hard, and accomplish great things.

Conversely, a woman who finds fault with a man and belittles him can cause him to rebel and to use his natural aggression to quarrel or destroy, eventually causing him to become ineffective in dealing with the world around him.

Encouragement can be as simple as a smile, a hug or a pat on the back. A boy gets a thrill when a girl he likes smiles at him or touches him. Many daughters learn to wrap their fathers "around their little fingers." This they learned early in life when they believed that Daddy was a different kind of man who would respond to flattery, a hug and a smile.

It is frequently said that behind every successful man there is a good woman. This saying is generally true, except that there are some successful men who never married and some unsupportive wives.

The best way to hold a boy you like a lot is to be considerate. Let him know you enjoy his company. Let him date others if he wants his freedom. When he likes you well enough to return time and again without intimate sex, you can be reasonably sure he is falling in love.

Even when aware of their power over men, many women don't use it because they have been brought up to believe that it is not lady-like or honorable for a woman to try to influence a man. However, many young women nowadays are more aggressive and see no harm in forgetting tradition to attract a good man and build a happy life for both.

Love and Sex Talk

Love talk is necessary to communicate a mutual attraction between a boy and a girl, but such talk is frequently used irresponsibly. Therefore, a girl should accept love talk with considerable reservation until she has known the boy for some time.

Both boys and girls want love and, instinctively, want sexual gratification, but the priorities and hazards are different. Sexual attraction makes words of love flow easily. However, girls are primarily interested in love, while boys are more interested in sexual gratification and freedom from commitment. Many boys and men feel love talk is for women and is not masculine.

These facts explain why a young woman easily accepts love talk as being the whole truth and why a young man quickly drops a girlfriend who demands commitment even after she has granted him sexual favors. Every situation is different, and each girl must handle overly aggressive males as best she can. However, the following thoughts may help.

A boy who tells a girl he has dated only a few times that he loves her and asks her to "prove" her love for him is saying, in effect, "Honey, I love myself and want to indulge my sexual urges. Therefore it is up to you to lend me your body and risk your future happiness for my sexual gratification." However, that is not what he says.

What do you say if a boy presses you for more intimate behavior? Merely state your position: "I like being with you, Mike, but I'm just not ready for intense love-making." State *your* position, not your parent's or anyone else's. Ask him to prove his love by being a gentleman. The more responsible young men will take you at your word and back off.

You don't have to give him more specific reasons for turning him down. By selecting a specific reason, you give him an opening to argue. Eventually, you will run out of answers. Remember that boys like to WIN.

If you say you don't want to get pregnant, he will assure you that you won't and that he will marry you if you do. If you say you're afraid of getting AIDS, he will assure you he hasn't been "exposed."

If he calls you a square or a lesbian, be insulted and say: "No way. Take me home, please." If you liked him before he became so persistent or crude, try to keep control of the situation without losing your temper. Some boys feel they have to test to see how far they can go.

Never, NEVER, during early courtship, tell him you love him, even though you may feel you do. Tell him you like him a lot or enjoy his company. If he starts talking love, try to change the subject to something that will interest him, such as sports or school. If you can't find a common interest other than sex, you can be sure that a long-term relationship is an impossibility.

If he says you owe it to him to satisfy his sex urges because he has spent money on you, tell him you assumed he liked you and did not think he would expect sex in exchange for his money and company. Let him know that the price he wants for his company is too high and that you will not take his favors in the future. Another way to divert this kind of argument is to suggest going dutch (both paying).

A male wants to win, but doesn't want a girlfriend or mate who is easy to push around. It is no fun to win over a weak team (or person). Let him win in less important contests. Don't battle him on his terms, which might be physical, mental, or both, except as a last resort.

Don't make him angry unless all else fails. An angry unprincipled male can become violent. Most boys will give up early so they can continue to be friends, especially if you have known them for some time. Keep enough money in your purse for a taxi ride home.

Girls generally know that when they expose a lot of anatomy, they will definitely attract the attention of boys, whether for good or bad. This is normal instinctive action by girls and reaction by boys. Many girls don't realize they may be unconsciously sending an invitation to boys who are interested in them only for sexual gratification.

If a boy is allowed to feel intimate parts of a girl's anatomy, he will be much harder to control. Once passions are aroused, it is especially difficult to keep from going all the way.

If a teenage girl becomes intimate with a boy after a few dates, she is more likely to lose him than she is to gain a lover. Breaking up is especially painful for a girl who has been sexually involved with a boy. This is so, not only because he rejected her, but also because he said he loved her, she believed him and trusted her body to him. Then he betrayed her. Being betrayed may result in distrust of all boys, which hinders developing wholesome boy-girl relationships.

THOUGHTS FOR SEXUALLY ACTIVE GIRLS

If you are sexually active and have not been in trouble, does this indicate you have learned how to use your body to hold a fellow's "love" and protect yourself from harm? Not really. The next date might be the one that gets you into trouble. This kind of relationship seldom lasts.

There is a new fashion of "secondary virginity." The term describes the woman who has participated in sexual intercourse, but has decided this kind of life is not for her. She will wait until she marries and is really in love before getting involved again.

The reasons for discontinuing sexual activity are many, including:

(1) The girl, or a friend or friends, have suffered from gynecological problems, venereal disease or AIDS;

(2) Sexual experience, without the security of the true love of a husband, was disappointing and not the exhilarating experience depicted by movies, T.V., or books;

(3) She has a friend or classmate who became pregnant and was abandoned or had an abortion;

(4) She decided temporary sexual liaisons just weren't worth the risks.

You may believe that if you become pregnant, it will be relatively easy to get an abortion. There are many clinics that make abortion a relatively inexpensive operation and certainly much safer than in the days when it was illegal. Some women who have had abortions report no difficulty.

However the problems with abortion are less apparent. Abortion is a sensitive issue that evokes a wide difference of opinions, based on religious beliefs or legal theory. Such a decision is not easy.

Dr. Bernard Nathanson, OB Gyn, a former abortionist, said: "People do not understand that there are thousands of serious physical complications from abortion every year in this country." These complications include physical problems during and immediately after the abortion and problems with conception many years later.

From Vincent Rue, Ph. D., a psychologist: "Abortion has a painful aftermath, regardless of the woman's religious beliefs or how positive she may have felt before and about her decision to abort."

From a teen-ager: "After my abortion, I just tried to go on living a teen-ager's life, but I was really depressed. I dreamed about the baby. I started hating myself for what I had done." Another person reported horrible nightmares about babies and people "trying to kill me."

It is obvious that there are strong instinctive physical and emotional reactions to abortion. Remember that reproductive instincts are powerful forces, and most women will have some psychological reactions.

In some instances, abortion may seem to be the only solution to a difficult problem, but there are alternatives.

To help women, both married and unmarried, who become pregnant and feel they can't afford a baby, there is an organization with chapters in most large cities called BIRTHRIGHT. It is staffed by volunteers who offer a confidential person to person approach of loving assistance to any woman regardless of age, marital status, race, religion, or economic status.

They offer free pregnancy tests, information on abortion alternatives, medical care for poor mothers, and much practical assistance. If the woman decides to put the baby up for adoption, referral is made to a good agency. If the decision is to keep the baby, Birthright helps young mothers stay in school, find work, temporary housing, and clothes.

Hotline numbers for Birthright and Planned Parenthood, a pro-choice organization, are provided in Appendix A.

There is no perfect solution to an unwanted pregnancy other than abstinence, so: SAVE YOUR LOVE FOR A SPOUSE, DON'T GIVE IT TO A LOUSE.

AVOIDING DATE RAPE

Television and movies frequently show a reluctant girl suddenly melt when an aggressive male grabs her for a smothering kiss. As a result, some irresponsible males interpret a woman's "No," as "Yes" and believe all girls react this way.

One survey reported that one out of four women in college were victims of rape or attempted rape between the ages of 14 and 21. In a survey of college males, three out of ten said they would force a woman to have sex if they could get away with it. One-third of college fraternity members in another survey said they felt a girl owed sexual favors in return for a good time.

All indications are that such attitudes and incidents are increasing. Therefore, Grandpop is passing on information learned from authorities in order to help young women avoid date rape.

Rape is a crime of violence, whether it be street rape or date rate. According to one authority, "Any incarcerated rapist will tell you that anger and power, not lust, were his reasons. The idea that anyone is asking to be raped because of her clothes is completely ludicrous."

Some experts believe that fewer than 5% of date rapes are reported to police. Reasons for failing to report date rape are various. Some women think that it was partially their fault and that people will think they were stupid for letting it happen. Another is the embarrassment caused by reporting intimate and frightening details to police and in court. The victims know it is difficult to obtain a conviction if the jury believes the girl cooperated up to a point.

So how should young women act to prevent date rape? Debra Roberts, a Gwinnett County, Ga. crime prevention specialist, suggests:

"(1) On the first date with a virtual stranger, the woman should pay her own way. Some rapists believe that if they spend money on a woman they have a right to expect to have sex with her.

"(2) A woman has to be firm and assertive. If the guy brings up the subject of sex and your answer is "No," be sure you say "No" in a way that is clear and unambiguous."

"(3) Physical resistance should be attempted only if the woman is sure she can inflict a disabling injury on her attacker. Eighty-five percent of the women who try to fight their attackers get injured, in addition to being raped."

"(4) Avoid being alone with a date in a se-cluded apartment or house, and don't drink. Data on date rape cases show that alcohol is almost always a factor, but it usually is the victim, rather than the perpetrator, who has been drinking."

"(5) Report the attack to police or a rape crisis center immediately. Some women think they can get through the aftermath of a rape on their own, but, in reality, most of them can't and will need professional help."

The best defense is an offense. Act as though you can't believe he is anything but a gentleman. Try not to show fear and don't fight back--except as a last resort. This is difficult in a fearsome situation.

Other ways to avoid rape include: (1) Yelling if people are within hearing distance; (2) Steering clear of overly aggressive males who seem resentful or inconsiderate of other people's feelings; (3) Setting limits and telling him early in the date; (4) Demanding to be taken home if he becomes angry or makes discourteous remarks; and (5) Dating only men and boys introduced by someone you can trust.

Well-balanced males see women as special friends rather than sex objects. Responsible men treat women with respect and affection. They control sexual drive and consider all rapists enemies of society.

ACTION SECTION

Make a list of things you are willing to do on dates and things to avoid. After each item, write down a reason. Put both lists in your Take Charge binder. It will be useful for reviewing when you start dating someone new.

CHAPTER VII

Making and Keeping Friends

Most of us tend to take friendship for granted and expect others to be friendly in much the same manner as we expect the sun to come up and our parents to love us. Extroverts seem to know how to make friends instinctively. Others learn from parents and friends.

People who make an effort to make friends are not only happier, but also more successful. All of us want to have many close friends, but few of us make a special effort to get people to like us. Part of the problem is not being adequately motivated to make the effort.

IMPORTANCE OF FRIENDSHIPS

To feel whole and happy, humans need to share the ups and downs of living with other people. In good times, we need others to talk to, laugh with, and share with. The fun phase takes little effort.

Friends will help you find dates and recommend other fun things to do. Friends will give you interests that you didn't know you had. They will help you with all kinds of problems, including school work, and will keep you from getting bored. There is a good chance that you will meet your future wife or husband through a friend.

After you finish school, the best opportunities in life will come through friends. Friends will not only tell you about job opportunities, but also will help you take advantage of them

In times of trial, we need people to sympath-ize, support, encourage and render assistance. Friends give us strength to go on with life in spite of problems.

Being alone is a miserable feeling. It results in boredom and depression. This frequently happ-ens to people who haven't learned to make friends easily or who go to work in a strange city.

Some people get depressed even when there are other people around who care. If this becomes mental illness, they have difficulty making decisions and must depend on friends and family to get them the help they need. Without help, their situations can become hopeless.

Here is a principle to remember: *NO MAN IS AN ISLAND.* What does that mean? It means we are surrounded by people, and we can't survive without help from one another. Each of us needs the help of parents, friends, and teachers. Your parents provide the basic security you need; friends provide the fun; and teachers provide the knowledge you need to become self-supporting.

It pays to make friends with adults of all ages. You never know when one will come to your assistance when you are in need. Many a poor young man or young woman has been helped through college by an older person who knew him or her to be honest and hard-working. The bene-factor may be a relative--or a friend who is willing to provide money for educational expenses.

In Chapter One, I told you about my bleak prospects of getting a college education. Now I will tell you how friends helped me get started on a successful career.

The publisher of a weekly newspaper in our county seat knew me slightly and heard I was try-ing to save enough money to go to business school. Without my knowing it, he made a deal with the school to trade advertising for my tuition, and he induced its staff to find a job to cover my room and board. After I was graduated, I paid him back out of my first paychecks.

I became friendly with the teachers and the president of the college. They helped me find a good-paying job. This was in the heart of the Great Depression when few jobs were available.

That job was teletype operator with a major news organization. I wasn't eligible for advancement since I did not have a journalism degree, but my boss found me a job as a country newspaper editor. The paper won several awards while I was there. Even then the future looked bleak without a college degree, so I looked for a change.

Again, a friend stepped in and found me a job. Odd though it may seen, I met this man literally by accident. The brakes on my car were faulty, and, in a minor collision, a small dent was made in his fender. It developed that he knew my brother. We worked out the repairs satisfactorily and later played cards together a few times.

When a vacancy occurred in the life insurance company where he was an officer, he recommended me for the job. Within three months I became his assistant, doing work that would normally have required a college degree. I changed companies three times, each time moving up until, eventually, I became a senior vice president. Of course dependability, hard work, and learning about the business were also factors in my success. However, friendship was always the door opener.

During my career, when my last company was still small with less than 100 home office employees, I did the hiring of all employees, except agents and top officers. Here are some facts I learned about friendships that will be useful to you when you seek employment.

We encouraged our employees to recruit their friends because good workers don't recommend people who aren't trustworthy and good workers. Finding a qualified stranger through advertisements and public sources is time consuming and risky. It is difficult for employers to get reliable references on people they don't know. Many of the better jobs aren't advertised because employers need people they can trust. However, we did advertise where special experience was required.

When hiring inexperienced clerical employees and secretaries, we depended heavily on interviews, tests, and calls to teachers and counselors. Obviously friendship with teachers, ministers and other responsible people is very helpful to both the applicant and the employer.

No one can make progress in the work situation who isn't friendly with nearly everyone. People in responsible positions may have to discharge those who don't give a fair day's work for a day's pay; but they get best results by being friendly and kind to the good workers.

Here is another principle to remember: *FRIENDSHIPS ARE IMPORTANT TO A HAPPY AND SUCCESSFUL LIFE.* You need to know how to make friends with all kinds of people and keep friendships alive in order to benefit from them.

The friends you make in school may just be pleasant memories after you finish school, but the *ability you develop to make friends* will stay with you and help you throughout life. Now is the time when you not only should be learning how friendships are built, but also making many of them.

ATTRACTING FRIENDS

Being attractive to others involves:
(1) Being as physically attractive as possible;
(2) Acting poised and confident; and
(3) Being a leader.

Being Physically Attractive

Being neat and clean usually doesn't seem important to most teen-agers. This is not as important in high school, where you have many friends, as it will be later in life when you are looking for members of the opposite sex to date or when you are looking for jobs.

Remember how proud you are of yourself when you have new clothes, you have just bathed, your hair is combed and in place (or your face make-up on) and you are ready to go out.

If you were born with good looks and a good build, you are fortunate. These factors do make a person more attractive. However, everyone's attractiveness can be improved with good diet, exercise, and sufficient sleep.

Many people are overweight. Those who haven't learned the importance of being kind and considerate frequently make disparaging remarks that lower the self-esteem of the overweight person. The latter then becomes defensive and eats more, further aggravating the situation.

Unless there is a glandular problem, most people can get personal weight under control and improve attractiveness by developing enough self-discipline and self-respect to control his or her eating habits. Ways of developing self-discipline were discussed in Chapter III

Getting an adequate amount of sleep also helps people be attractive. An adequate amount of sleep varies, but doctors generally agree that eight hours is sufficient for most adults and teens.

People who get enough sleep are more alert and more sensitive to others, and their eyes are brighter. Without enough sleep, judgment is faulty, quality of work suffers, and a person seems dull. Studying for long hours with only a few hours of sleep not only reduces a student's effectiveness, but also makes him or her irritable and critical of others. It is best to relax an hour or two during long periods of study and to go to bed on schedule.

ACTING poised and confident

Notice that the word "acting" in this subtitle is capitalized. Anyone can be an actor of sorts. Most small children who throw a tantrum are really acting. Experience has taught them this can get them attention from parents.

Acting in a situation that promotes good will is not being dishonest. In fact, people who act enthusiastic become enthusiastic, and people who act sympathetic actually find that they are sympathetic and concerned.

ACTING confident means holding your head up and being alert. If you sulk and hang your head, people will avoid you in the way you would avoid a dog who sneaks around with his tail between his legs. The dog may have been abused to lose his feeling of self-worth, but you are smarter and can control how you act.

If a dog comes up to you wagging it's tail, wouldn't you smile and pet it? Likewise, if you act confident and friendly, most people will be friendly to you. Expect a few grouches, but don't let them ruin your day.

Some young people, and even some adults, are very cruel to those who are timid and easily upset. Their subconscious minds are telling them if they put someone else down, they are elevating themselves. Instead, they are really broadcasting their own insecurity.

If you suffer some rebuffs and humiliation while trying to make friends, keep on trying. Don't be discouraged. A baby must crawl before it can walk. It must walk and fall down a few times before it can run.

If someone is unkind to you, act calm and poised. Instead of fighting back with words or fists, say something like, "Have a good day, Joe." Joe might even apologize to you. If he continues to give you trouble, don't ignore him. He wants attention. It might be more appropriate to talk to him, changing the subject.

It may take some acting to exude confidence because most teen-agers are somewhat insecure. This is natural because they know there is a lot they don't know. Try not to worry about what others think of you. Just do the best you can and expect some unkind treatment.

If you make a mistake and people laugh at you, laugh with them. They'll like you better. They didn't mean to be impolite. What you did struck them as being funny. Laughter is a tension reliever and a technique for dealing with embarrassment. If you fight back, it will spoil the fun for both of you.

It never hurts to say you are sorry, but do it sincerely and simply. Don't apologize profusely for mistakes unless you have obviously grievously hurt or offended someone.

Give the impression to others through your actions that you feel equal to, but not superior, to them. Pride in self is reflected in a humble and kindly behavior and an attitude that breeds respect.

Be a Leader

You can be a leader without running for class president. Just take the initiative when something needs attention. Most people respect those who have the courage to speak up when they see a wrong being committed or about to be committed. This is as true of teen-agers as it is of adults.

Usually a few students set the standards for most of the student body. Although young people want to be more independent with their family relationships, they tend to conform in peer relationships. They tend to dress alike and act alike. There is nothing wrong with belonging to the group and being friendly. It can, however, indicate an unwillingness to be different for fear of being laughed at or belittled.

Here is a principal: *DARE TO BE A LEADER.*

SHOWING AN INTEREST IN OTHERS

We are all curious about a new face, but we tend to be hesitant about striking up a conversation lest we get rebuffed. Go ahead and satisfy your curiosity, without being unkind. It is a rare oituation when anyone, particularly a young person, gives a short answer to someone who seems interested in him or her.

Ways to show an interest in a person include:

(1) Smile and touch frequently;
(2) Introduce yourself;
(3) Remember and use names;
(4) Ask questions; and
(5) Be a good listener.

Smile and Touch

Smile or wave at people even though you know them only slightly. A smile is a universal sign of friendship. It is like sunshine or throwing out a welcome mat. People might be shy and are looking for an opening to talk to you. A smile invites people to speak and be friendly.

Handshakes, touching and hugging also are acceptable ways of showing friendship. Putting an arm around the shoulders of a friend to compliment him or her or to show sympathy is nearly always appreciated. Men usually shy away from hugging each other, preferring a handshake.

Don't hug people you know only slightly. In such a situation, a handshake or a pat on the hand or back is more appropriate.

KEEP ON SMILING AND BEING FRIENDLY. It will make your day and send out a warm glow to everyone around you.

Introduce yourself

When you get a chance to talk to someone-- even when standing in line--introduce yourself. If you are with friends who are carrying on an animated conversation, they won't miss you if you start talking to someone else.

During introductions, look the person in the face, SMILE and enunciate your name carefully, spelling it if it is unusual. Shake hands firmly, but don't squeeze. Repeat the name when you say you are glad to meet him or her. This will help you remember it.

The person who looks down or mumbles his or her name gives the impression he or she isn't interested in knowing you and won't be remembered.

Talking to strangers in schools, churches and other places your friends normally go should cause no problem. Talking to a person in a theater or other public place can ease tension and should be no problem if you don't try to develop the friendship further.

Remember And Use Names

Everyone likes to be recognized and likes to hear his or her name. Use it frequently. This will impress it on your memory and the person will be much more friendly to you in the future.

Here is a trick for remembering last names. Associate the name with a picture or fact. For example, a foreign name like Lucyk can be remembered by thinking of the person as lucky. Reznicek can be remembered as raising a check over his head or a raisin lying on a check. These are close enough so you can adjust to the correct pronunciation.

Don't ever get too embarrassed to ask a person for a second or third time about his name. Usually a person will be flattered that you are trying to remember his or her name.

Although young people like to be called by their first names, adults prefer and will be more polite to you if you use last names and Mr., Mrs., Miss, or Ms.

Ask Questions

There are many ways to start a conversation: Ask questions about classes, teachers or activities. Comment on the weather, the sports teams, the upcoming party or dance, or any subject of general interest. Compliment clothes or achievements. Inquiring about health, if the person has been sick or away, shows personal interest.

If you ask questions, give the reply your undivided attention. If you let your attention wander, you will appear to be uninterested and rude. Unless your questions reflect a sincere desire to know, stick to light conversation.

Be A Good Listener

Perhaps you have noticed that the nicest people are those who ask you questions and listen to your answers. We all notice beautiful and handsome people, but those who seem to have charisma are those who notice us and listen. If you do as they do, you will have many friends.

Avoid talking about yourself extensively. People who talk endlessly about themselves are boring because they give the impression they are more interested in themselves than in the listener. If the person finds out about your accomplishments from someone else, he or she will be far more impressed than if you mention them yourself.

If a person asks you questions, by all means answer and make it sound like you appreciate the person's interest. It doesn't hurt to mention a coincidence or something you have in common and to sound excited about it. If the person is interested, he or she will ask for more details, in which case you will establish a special bond with that person.

MAINTAINING FRIENDSHIPS

Simply stated we maintain friendships by being kind and considerate.

There are too many ways to be kind and considerate to attempt an itemization. They involve the heart, emotions and mind. Each situation is different. Here are a few of the more important things to remember:

(1) Accept people as they are,
(2) Be loyal,
(3) Congratulate and sympathize,
(4) Forgive people who have offended you,
(5) Spare feelings when possible,
(6) Avoid antagonizing people,
(7) Don't gossip or bad-mouth others, and
(8) Don't keep score.

Accept People As They Are

We all have faults, so don't be picky. Even if you aren't particularly attracted to a person, it doesn't cost anything to be nice. Later, you may find a hidden beauty that you didn't sense at first.

Avoid "putting someone down" because he or she is different or poor in worldly possessions. Accept the fact that no one is perfect.

The poor may have lacked opportunities or started lower and had a harder time pulling themselves up. Part of it may be bad luck, as in the case of teen-agers who were pulled into life's whirlpool through sex, liquor or drugs. Of course, some avoided responsibility or couldn't be trusted, so they were bypassed when opportunities became available.

Some of those who get into trouble may have parents who give them too much money or freedom, or parents who give them nothing, not even love. They may not have developed self-discipline and just drifted. Yet, they need to have friends as much as you and I. Most of them are nice people when they are in a relaxed situation.

Christ said, "What you do to the least of my brothers, that you do unto me." To be a happy person, you need to be proud of what you are and have been able to accomplish. You also must tolerate and help those less fortunate. In school, that means helping those who are slow learners, or at least, being nice and not ridiculing them, making fun of them or giving them a hard time. One of them might be your boss someday.

Be Loyal

Keep confidences and stand up for your friends when they need help. If someone tells you something in confidence, it means that person considers you to be a special friend who can be trusted. If you betray that confidence, you may lose a special friend.

Congratulate and Sympathize:

Compliment frequently. Share praise and give credit to others in mutual achievements. Don't be afraid to be the first or last person to praise, but be sincere. People are always hungry for recognition and praise. The more recognition you give others, the more friendly and helpful they will be.

When you congratulate someone, ACT enthusiastic, or if you offer sympathy, ACT sympathetic. Words are more meaningful if you say them with the appropriate emotional emphasis.

Forgive people who have offended you

If someone has offended you and you have quarrelled with that person, it will be difficult for you to forgive him or her. It will be equally difficult for the other person to forgive you.

Each time you see each other, the hurt will be renewed. The quarrel may continue and get worse unless one of you tries to make peace. Even if you didn't say mean things, you won't be at peace until you have made an effort to reconcile your differences.

You may find that the person was upset about something or someone else and didn't mean to be snippy or argumentative. Also you may have misinterpreted something that was said. The more you understand why a person acts a certain way, the less irritated you will be.

Have you ever said something in a fit of anger or jealousy to hurt someone? Of course, you have. Didn't you later regret it? But did you go out of your way to apologize? Probably not, because you because you were too embarrassed to admit to yourself and friends that you didn't mean it. Only forgiveness and love can erase ill feelings. So why not be big about it, say you were upset, and said things you didn't mean. Ask for forgiveness and tell the person you want to be friends.

Here's a PRINCIPLE to remember. *"I'M SORRY", "PLEASE FORGIVE ME", AND "I FORGIVE YOU" ARE POWERFUL PHRASES FOR MAKING PEACE WITH YOURSELF AND OTHERS.*

Spare Feelings When Possible

Don't say anything negative or critical unless you are certain that speaking out will be acceptable. If so, cushion the blow as much as possible.

Many times we have to tell a person bad news or much-needed, constructive criticism. Telling a lie in such a case is unkind. When the person learns the truth, he or she will become upset with you and you could lose a friend. It is better to tell the truth in a way that lessens the hurt. One way is to use the sandwich method, which is putting the negative in between two positive statements.

If a person asks your opinion, it usually is a good idea to say something like, "I haven't made up my mind. What do you think?" In this manner you can find out how the person stands. If you disagree and it is not important, you have avoided an argument.

If you strongly disagree, go ahead and state your position, and ask the other person why he or she thinks differently. Asking reasons indicates friendship and an open mind. This also avoids an emotional argument. If you agree, you then can speak freely.

Avoid making wisecracks or jokes about things that are more or less beyond a person's control. This includes his or her name, skin color, complexion, and facial and body features. These jokes create resentment and sometimes detract from the person's feeling of self-worth.

Avoid Antagonizing People

Antagonizing people makes enemies. You probably won't know it when someone you have offended harms you, such as keeping you from receiving an honor you have earned or giving you a bad recommendation.

Very little is accomplished by arguing in a social situation. Arguing can turn a friend into an enemy. Many divorces result from arguments that started over something unimportant and ended in unjustified personal remarks hard to forgive.

If the argument is about religion or politics, no one wins since both sides usually have closed minds, having read, heard, and thought a great deal about the subject in the past.

People hate to admit they are wrong. The person who wins an argument may lose a friend. The exception is the person who likes to argue for argument;s sake. He likes to win, but wants to compete with someone he considers his equal.

If a person makes insulting remarks or gets emotional and won't let you change the subject, control your temper. It is better to turn your back and refuse to talk than to continue the discussion. Later, he or she may apologize.

The suggestions in this chapter apply to making friends of either sex. However, there is one additional thought for boys. Most girls aren't comfortable around boys who make sexist or crude remarks. If a girl wants to listen to this kind of conversation, she will let you know in a subtle way. Don't interpret a smile as an invitation to be crude.

Here's a principle to remember: *ONE   ENEMY CAN DO YOU MORE HARM THAN A HUNDRED FRIENDS CAN DO GOOD.*

Don't Gossip or Bad Mouth Others

People who speak unpleasantly about others give a bad impression about the subject and about themselves. If the gossip is scandalous and it later proves untrue, you are harming an innocent person. If it is true and the person finds out what you have said, you will have an enemy.

Don't Keep Score

If you want to keep friends, forget what you give and remember only what you receive. If a person offers to do something for you that requires effort or a nominal expense they can easily afford, accept it graciously. Don't refuse because you feel you will owe something in return or because it hurts your pride. Some people want to help and are hurt when their help is rejected.

If you get a birthday or Christmas present, you don't owe one in return unless you can afford one and want to give one. What you must do is write a gracious thank-you note. This applies to relatives, as well as good friends.

GETTING ALONG WITH TEACHERS

The most important adults in your life, other than your parents, are your teachers. Your future success and happiness depend on the knowledge you receive from them.

Men and women become teachers because they love being involved with other people, particularly young people. They delight in seeing young people grow in knowledge and maturity.

Teachers love their work when students co-operate. They try to impress upon students that studying is not a waste of time, and they become distressed by those who think goofing off is funny.

They care about you and want to help you. This is a form of love.

Teachers get paid for teaching, but this doesn't compensate for the rudeness of some students. Most teachers could earn more money with less aggravation if they took commercial jobs.

The fact that you may find school work difficult is not the teachers' fault. If you faithfully completed your assignments in the past, you should find school work challenging and interesting. There are ways to correct your learning deficiencies if you seek them out.

There are two ways to make friends with a teacher. Compliment the teacher on how interesting and thoroughly he or she covered a particular subject. We all like to be praised, even teachers. If you praise a teacher for his or her work, be sincere. If you didn't study and are trying to get a good grade by flattery, you will lose credibility and alienate the teacher.

The second way to make friends with a teacher is to be an eager and hard-working student. Asking the teacher for more sources of information on subjects being studied also is helpful. The teacher will probably feel adequately rewarded if you accept and follow suggestions.

Don't tell a teacher of the opposite sex that you love him or her. You may mean that your love is the same as it is for all good people, but there is so much puppy love by students for teachers that such conversation could be embarrassing to the teacher.

Here is a quote from Abigail Van Buren's column that very simply summarizes the contents of this chapter:

"The key to being popular with both sexes is: Be kind. Be honest. Be tactful. If you can't be beautiful (or handsome), be well-groomed, tastefully attired, conscious of your posture and *KEEP A SMILE ON YOUR FACE.*

"Be clean in body and mind. If you're not a 'brain,' try harder. If you're not a great athlete, be a good sport. Try to be a standout in something. If you can't dance or sing, learn to play an instrument. Think for yourself, but respect the rules. Be generous with kind words and affectionate gestures, but save the heavy artillery for later. You'll be glad you did. If you need help, ask God. If you don't need anything, thank God."

There are many thoughts in this chapter on making friends, but we can summarize them by saying, **"If you want to be popular, be kind, friendly, and enthusiastic."**

ACTION SECTION

List in your Take Charge binder the following tasks:

(1) Make at least one new friend each day for at least 30 days. On a separate sheet, describe how you plan to proceed. Don't plan a party, but take advantage of opportunities that present themselves daily.

An example: "I will introduce myself to a different person in my English class each day until I know every one by his or her first name and know the things he or she likes to do."

Don't worry that fellow students will think you are pushy. Just tell them you are trying to get to know everyone in class. You might be amazed with how friendly they will react.

Keep track of the names of your new friends, with a separate sheet of paper for each, showing the date you met each person, what he or she does in the way of school activities, and something personal about him or her, such as hobbies. Try to include equal numbers of both sexes.

(2) Tell a different teacher each day for a week that you appreciate what he or she does for you.

(3) This is an exercise to help you build confidence in yourself. On a sheet of paper, list all of the good things in your life including your good qualities. On another sheet, list all of the bad things about yourself that you don't like or which parents, teachers and others occasionally criticize.

Go through the list of negatives and decide what you can do about them. Transfer those that can be corrected, or substantially changed, to your Take Charge list, but leave off dates when you will begin to remedy them. That can come later. Now cross these off the negative list, leaving only the negatives you must accept.

Make a list of other people, especially friends, who also have similar negatives. If these don't seem to bother your relationship with those friends, cross them off the negative list. Compare the positive and negative lists.

This comparison should make you realize you have more good things in life and more good qualities than bad. With a little effort applied to correct the items on the Take Charge list, you can become a very nice person to know.

CHAPTER VIII

Family Relationships

Probably more hours per week are spent in a home atmosphere than anywhere else. Therefore, it is wise to make a special effort to make family relationships as pleasant as possible.

You are indeed fortunate if you live in a home with two parents who frequently assure you of their love, who always speak softly to each other, and who agree on all matters affecting you. Such ideal conditions are rare.

If you have such an ideal situation and you have no brothers or sisters, much of this chapter will not apply to you. However, some parts dealing with friction will be helpful in planning for the future.

IMPORTANCE OF FAMILY

Children of all ages take their family situation for granted in much the same way as we take water for granted. No one appreciates water until the well runs dry. Likewise, children don't appreciate family until parents divorce or die.

Children expect parents to be there when needed. Your parents were with you at birth and most of the time since. Some day you will probably be a parent and will understand and appreciate the many obstacles and challenges your mother and father faced, individually, and as a part of the family.

If you live in a two-parent home, consider yourself fortunate even if there is friction. One young man was complaining to a friend about his father yelling at him.   The friend commented, "I wish I had a father to yell at me."

There will come a day when your parents will be in bad health and will depend upon you.   Then, family will become as meaningful and important to your parents, as it is to you now.   There also will come a day when you may be dependent upon your children.   You will be glad that you had children and gave them your whole-hearted love.

In the last chapter, we pointed out the importance of friends in times of trial.   Friends come and go, but family ties are more permanent.   In times of trouble, families usually are the only source of real help.   When there is serious illness and death, friends give sympathy, but family members give real support.   They unselfishly spend nights at the bedside and nurse sick relatives back to health and give financial help when it is sorely needed.

Much has appeared in the media about the **disappearance of family life.**   It hasn't disappeared, but it has changed, with more and more single parent homes, more diversiond, and poorer communication between family members.

There are many reasons for the change including: television; easy availability of divorce; fewer lifetime commitments in marriage; a greater interest in recreational sex; and more working mothers whose time for family interaction is limited.

If your life is to be happy, you must get along well with and help your parents, brothers, and sisters so your home will be a wonderful relaxing place.   Of course, you can't do it by yourself, but you can make a difference if you work at being an unselfish, loving son or daughter, brother or sister.   People who turn their backs on family relationships will pay a price.

DEALING WITH PARENTS

Most modern parents are too busy to spend much time communicating with their teen-age children. This is especially true when both work. The lure of television, teens' struggles for independence, more outside activities and easy access to automobiles are contributing factors.

Sometimes, teen-agers revert to childlike behavior to get what they want. This causes a parent to treat them as small children, causing resentment. Children grow up so gradually, it is difficult for parents to recognize that a child is rapidly becoming a young adult with a mind of his or her own. If you make requests calmly, you will have a better chance of getting what you want.

Parents are human like you and I. They have emotions, needs and desires. They make mistakes and, at times, are selfish. However, they have more experience in life situations, give you security, and they love you. Therefore, unless your parents are immoral or extremely abusive, you should accept your parents' decisions even when you feel they are being unfair.

Dealing with parents will be discussed in three parts:
(1) Demonstrating Affection;
(2) Earning Trust; and
(3) Minimizing Friction.

Demonstrating Affection

The mating or reproductive instinct is just as strong, if not stronger, in your parents as it is in you. It frequently is as important, or more important, to them than the love for their children. However, love for a mate and love for children should be interrelated. After all, your parents' love for each other came before you were born.

You probably don't want to think anyone is more important than you, but, if you do your part to make your family life happy, you will have less worry about security and future happiness.

All of us need to be assured by actions and words that we are loved, appreciated, and respected. Some men and a few women find it difficult to show affection because their parents showed them little or no affection when they were growing up. Children who get no affection have difficulty showing affection to others. Some men feel showing affection isn't masculine unless they want sex.

If you have difficulty expressing affection, your difficulty will increase with age and cause marital problems unless corrected while you are young and more flexible. Both boys and girls can build a happier home life by making a special effort to show affection.

You can practice showing affection by: (1) telling your parents how much you appreciate what they do for you; (2) telling them how much you love them; (3) giving them occasional hugs; and (4) helping them without being asked.

It's much easier for parents to give in to a child who says he or she loves the parent and voluntarily helps around the house. Remember there is a price to pay for all happiness.

To love parents means accepting them as they are. Many prominent scientists, professional people, artists, and public leaders came from simple homes and simple parents. Intelligence, education, and kindness depend largely upon the opportunities they had to learn while growing up. You can't make parents smarter or more understanding by criticizing and finding fault. You will only make yourself and them unhappy.

Parents want to be proud of their children and love them regardless of their behavior. Love them because they love you. They provide shelter, food, clothing, education, and love until a child can pay his or her own way. Therefore, parents' opinions should be honored, and they should have the final authority. Remember the commandment: *HONOR THY FATHER AND THY MOTHER.*

One young man made this observation: "When I was fourteen, I thought my Dad was dumb. But when I became 21, I was amazed at how much he had learned in those seven years." Obviously, the father had not changed. The son had gained understanding.

Earning Trust

Teen-agers are usually vaguely aware that their parents love them and mean well. But the young people ask, "How can you become responsible if your parents second guess everything you do? Parents are always wanting to know where you are going and when you will be back. They won't let you watch certain TV programs, won't buy you your own automobile, and won't even let you use the family car when you need it. They also deprive you in many other ways."

If you feel this way, ask yourself whether you always tell your parents about your plans. Have you been in trouble because you did something they warned you against? Trust is based on credibility and experience. If you find you can rely on what someone says, you will usually trust them. Parents are no different, but they tend to be overly cautious. Mothers worry a lot because they love their children and don't want them to get into trouble.

There probably have been times in your life when your parents or teachers promised something, but didn't keep the promise. Perhaps, they told you something you found wasn't true. They probably had a good reason, but remember how frustrated and angry you became?

Your parents become equally frustrated when you break promises or tell lies. The only way to earn trust is to build credibility by keeping promises and being truthful. Here's a principle to remember: *FOR A HAPPIER HOME LIFE, ACCEPT RESPONSIBILITY*

Minimizing Friction

If your parents quarrel a lot, you'll feel insecure and, possibly, guilty. Even though your parents quarrel about your discipline, wants, or needs, it isn't your fault unless you threw a tantrum to get what you wanted.

There is no way you can prevent these conflicts. You can minimize your demands and assure both parents that you love them and hate it when they have these differences.

Try to find a time each day when you can chat with family members. After school is a good time to talk to brothers and sisters, but mealtimes is best for family discussions. Relaxed conversations bring a family closer together and facilitate discussion of important issues.

NEVER get one parent to handle your problems with the other. You may get your way for the moment, but you will pay the price later through strained relationships in the home. By the time you become an adult, you will need to learn how to persuade people. Why not practice on parents?

When you have something on your mind that is very important to you, try to pick a time when your mother or father is usually in a good mood and ask to talk for five minutes. This might be after a good meal, while helping with a chore or while going for a walk or ride. Have your thoughts written down so you can present them smoothly.

If your parent or parents demand to know what you want to talk about, explain briefly, but ask for the opportunity to sit down so you won't feel rushed. If the parent declines to set a time, let it drop for the time being and try again the next day with a different approach and more thorough justification. Chances are the parent will give in and admire the mature way you handled the situation.

If either of you gets emotional or loses his or her "cool", postpone further discussions. Tell your parent or parents you love them, will try to understand them. End with a hug.

Teen-agers who get into trouble frequently may be rebelling against an overly strict parent. They may not realize that they are rebelling, but they go ahead impulsively to do something they have been warned about, throwing caution to the winds.

If you feel a parent is excessively dominant, try unloading your problems on a sympathetic counselor, minister, teacher, or understanding relative. Before you seek help, write down the facts so that emotion won't overcome you. Remember that when EMOTION COMES IN THE DOOR, JUDGMENT GOES OUT THE WINDOW.

Many times, a counselor can't help you, but discussing the problem with an understanding person may make you see a solution. You may realize you were unreasonable or may come up with a good way to resolve the problem yourself.

RELATIONSHIPS WITH BROTHERS AND SISTERS

Children from large families adjust much easier to the outside world. They learn early that if there is to be peace, there must be give and take.

Even in the best families, there is some strife. We are all competitive, and we see the world as it affects us individually. To some extent, conflict helps children develop enough dominance to protect themselves against "being walked on," inside and outside the family circle.

As family, we tend to stick together when dealing with outsiders, but, when dealing with others in the family circle, we tend to concentrate on our own personal wants.   Resentment among children can lead them to say they hate each other. This is usually not true, but is something said impulsively and in frustration.   We do want peace, but we usually don't work at it as much as we should for maximum family unity.

Developing concern for and love for a brother or sister will bring you many rewards.   If you develop a good relationship while you live in the same house, you and your brothers and sisters can and will continue to be good friends for life.

Most of the suggestions in the last chapter for maintaining friendships apply to family relationships.   Here are some specific suggestions for improving relations with parents and brothers and sisters:

(1) Don't dominate.   Make your point by asking questions.
(2) Be willing to say you are wrong when losing will not result in material harm to anyone else.
(3) Hug anyone who does something for you.
(4) Use the phrase, "I love you" frequently.
(5) Pray for others and pray for guidance for yourself.

PLANNING TO HAVE CHILDREN?

You may not want to answer this question now, but thinking about it now will help you better plan a good life.

Having children means sacrificing during the early married years to provide security and happiness in later years.   It means accepting responsibility for your life, your spouse, and future children.   Is it worth the cost?

The sheer wonder of a new baby and the instinctive love he or she inspires are just two of the joys of having children.   When a small child smiles at a parent and tries to talk, waving those tiny hands, all of the pains, discomforts, and cries in the night are forgotten.

Security is necessary to a happy life for a child and is provided by immediate family. It is easy to drift along through life, thinking only of self and accepting whatever comes. However, the best things come to those who plan wisely and unselfishly for the future and then make an effort to bring the plans to fruition.

Love for children can cause love for a mate to grow stronger. Remember the principle: *THE MORE LOVE YOU GIVE THE MORE YOU HAVE LEFT.*

The fact that parents are willing to accept responsibility for a family demonstrates unselfishness and love. Assuming a family stays together through old age, each parent will care for the other in time of stress. There will be a time when they can travel together and go to more social affairs.

Eventually, one's health will fail, and the other will be there to care for the invalid partner. When one dies, children who have been loved through the years will be there to offer care and moral and financial support to the surviving parent. If the family has had a loving relationship, the surviving partner might remarry, freeing the children from much responsibility. Parents who don't demonstrate affection can end up with children who are selfish and do not accept responsibility for parents in old age

Having a family is not all roses and honeysuckle. There are many ups and downs, but that comes with living and loving. Remember that a lifetime of happiness depends on consideration for others and is enhanced by generous helpings of love.

Mothers must go through the pains of childbirth. Every mother says the happiness the baby brought far outweighs the pain. Fathers who love their wives worry all through the pregnancy and birth period and share the mother's joy.

An insecure father may be temporarily jealous of the attention the child gets from the mother, but most babies bring the parents closer together. Talking to and playing with the child makes any adult feel more at ease with himself or herself and with the world.

The child requires a lot of attention, so the parents may stay home more and enjoy each other more. As the child grows and starts to school, they jointly thrill with the accomplishments of their son or daughter.

Parents who work hard and long hours may earn more money for the family to spend, but the work schedules can cause friction in the marriage and possibly divorce. This frequently happens when the father gets totally absorbed in his career while the mother takes sole responsibility for the children. He may feel he can't succeed unless he devotes more than 40 hours a week to the job.

Even though both parents get so busy they have little time for the children, families usually have many happy times together. Later in life, parents usually enjoy their roles as grandparents. They may have been too busy to enjoy the children in early years, but it seems they never get too old to enjoy grandchildren.

Many people want to have fun without responsibility or obligation. In the final analysis, there is no such thing. Let's look at the lives of Jim and Mary who married with the understanding they would not have children.

They justified their decision to remain childless on their view that the world is overpopulated and crime-ridden. The truth was they wanted freedom to spend their money on personal pleasure.

Instead of spending money for children's doctor bills, clothing, food, schooling, and allowances, they spent it at fancy restaurants, at bars, and on trips to exotic places. They slept late on weekends because there was no reason to get up and because of alcoholic hang-overs.

They started putting on weight from too much high life and joined a health club. They went several times but quit after a few weeks. It took too much effort, and they weren't dedicated to good health and genuine happiness.

Since they frequently went to parties with other couples who did not have children, they found many opportunities to have sex outside of their marriage. Since they were dedicated to self only, neither felt a strong attachment to the other. Divorce and other unhappiness soon followed.

They both remarried. Jim picked a young woman who attracted him by her charm and thoughtfulness. With the help of his new wife and Alcoholics Anonymous, he straightened out his life.

Mary had lost most of her good looks and figure during her marriage to Jim. She continued to drink, and her second marriage also ended in divorce. She cut back on her drinking because she had to resume working and, otherwise, couldn't hold a job.

She had no family except for a brother, who had disapproved of her life style. Her last years were spent in a nursing home with only an occasional visit from her sister-in-law.

Some couples would like to have children, but, for physical reasons, cannot. Since they are unselfish and want children, they have far fewer problems than those who are "non-parents by choice." In fact, many dedicated career people love their work as much as their mates and are happier working than raising children. They run a greater risk of ending up alone in old age than do parents.

ACTION SECTION

Here are some suggestions for cementing in your memory the many thoughts presented in this chapter:

(1) Enter on your Take Charge list that you will tell your parents at least once a month how much you appreciate what they do for you, how lucky you are to have such nice parents and how much you love them. Select a particular date of the month so you won't have trouble remembering. The idea is not to take parents for granted.

(2) Enter on your list a notation that on a certain day each month you will compliment your brothers and sisters, if any. The day of the month on which a birthday falls, or the first day of the month is a good date that is easy to remember.

CHAPTER IX

Divorce and Other Family Problems

When a family breaks up, the sudden loss of security panics the children. They may have to move away from their friends and go to live with a step-parent who is far less understanding than their birth mother or father. They also may feel guilty if they were rude and uncooperative, and may wonder if they aggravated their parents' problems. They suddenly appreciate what they had taken for granted.

There are many factors that lead to single parent families, divorce being the most likely. Sometimes a couple had sex before marriage and the man disappeared when she became pregnant. Sometimes, a career woman decides she wants a child without the responsibility of marriage.

Causes for divorce are many and varied. The children are rarely the cause. When parents decide to get a divorce, they are very concerned about what will happen to the children and, usually, both seek custody. This demonstrates that they care, but the bitterness between the adults may make the one who loses custody avoid the children.

Once a couple splits, there is little anyone, especially the children, can do to get them back together. The children must be accepting, understanding, and willing to acknowledge that both parents are still nice people. They can learn from their parents' mistakes and resolve to find a mate with ideas about life similar to their own.

If you live in a single parent home, don't blame the absence of one parent on the other.

Accept it and try to build a happy life for yourself, with or without help.

PARENTAL ROMANCES

Single parents are as sexually motivated, or more, than you are. It is normal for them to want to date. It also is normal for a teen-ager to be jealous of boyfriends or girlfriends of a single parent, but it is not good to let the jealousy destroy a parent's chance to remarry.

If you succeed in breaking them up, you will probably regret it later. After you leave home to marry or be on your own, your parent will be older and may be less attractive to the opposite sex. A woman, in particular, may have to live alone for the rest of her life or move in with you when her health deteriorates.

If you love your parent, you will be unselfish and try to find the best in his or her dates. If you really feel the person is not good for your parent, write down your reservations and talk about them sensibly and calmly. Many parents will not remarry if they feel their children will be harmed. However, if your reasons are based on jealousy, or if a parent is carried away with infatuation or love, it may be impossible to get him or her to listen.

This book does not get involved in adult relationships except where it affects you and other teen-agers. A broken home leaves the children with emotional scars that they can and must accept. By developing your own personality through self-discipline, challenging yourself, and achieving, you can build a happy future for yourself.

All of the problems that divorced parents and their children have should be a powerful incentive for you to keep your emotions from overruling your mind when you consider marrying or living with a boyfriend or girlfriend.

SERIOUS FAMILY PROBLEMS

If you have an alcoholic parent who is making life difficult, you can seek help from an organization called Alateen. Information in available from the Al-Anon chapters in most cities and the toll-free number in Appendix B.

An abusive situation may occur if you live with an alcoholic parent, step-parent, or your mother's boyfriend. Many other situations also can cause trouble.

If you are being physically or sexually abused, discuss the matter with an unbiased adult, such as a school counselor, minister, trusted teacher, or doctor. If that person feels your complaint is legitimate, he or she will make sure you receive help. It may not help to discuss the situation with relatives or neighbors because they may be reluctant to "get involved." Professionals consider it a part of their jobs.

Don't ever make abuse reports to get revenge. If authorities make a case, there is a strong possibility it will destroy your home and security. Life in a foster home might be easier than in your parent's home, but don't count on it unless life at home is unbearable. If authorities don't make a case, the offending parent or step-parent may be very resentful and your life will not improve.

Girls who marry to get out of an abusive home usually find that it was an unhappy and unsatisfactory solution. Marriages of convenience usually end in divorce, with even more unhappiness than the previous home situation, and, possibly, the added responsibility of a child.

Children who grow up together are not usually tempted to become romantically involved because of natural rivalry, parental supervision, and, probably, instinct. However, when couples divorce, remarry and merge families, that rivalry may not develop between the children. Teen-agers in such situations must recognize that any closer relationships, other than a brother-sister relationship, can be disastrous, and should be avoided. *It's hard to walk away from an infatuation or sexual relationship if the other person lives in the same house as you do.*

Sexual involvement between boys and girls in the same family is strictly prohibited by law and can cause problems galore. Your biological courses in school probably have taught you that children of close blood relatives are frequently born with deformities and mental problems.

If your home life ever gets so difficult that you plan to run away, try calling Covenant House, Boys Town, or one of the other toll-free numbers listed in Appendix B. These institutions work with both boys and girls. Life on the streets of a major city can be a nightmare.

If you feel so much stress that you don't want to talk to parents or friends and are even considering suicide, force yourself to call a suicide prevention number. Telephone information and long distance operators usually know the numbers of these services. In most cities, they can be found in the business directory. If not, contact the health departments, school counselors or ministers. These people are trained to help depressed people.

Once a person has taken his or her own life, there is no way to get it back. If a depressed person can find someone to listen to his cry for help and offer alternatives to suicide, he or she can still have a happy life. Someone, somewhere, should be able to help. Pray to have that person sent to you and make it easy for him or her to find you.

CHAPTER X

Following the Wrong Leader

Undoubtedly your parents and teachers have warned you about all of the problems discussed in this chapter. Nevertheless, some repetition, with stories dramatizing the ease with which one can take the wrong path, should do no harm. We also hope you find them interesting.

Most of the time, it is okay to be one of the crowd. Do as your friends do without rocking the boat. If everyone is dressing a certain way and parents and school authorities allow it, there is no harm in conforming. To do so may make you more acceptable to friends.

However, there are situations where following the leaders can be harmful to you. Think long and carefully before you let a casual acquaintance or friend induce you to do something you could regret for the rest of your life.

Surveys indicate that a very high percentage of teens have experimented with drugs, alcohol, and unprotected sex. Other surveys indicate that crimes committed by young adults also are increasing at a high rate.

Potential problems related to sex were discussed in an earlier chapter. Now for the less popular subjects.

STEALING AND DISHONESTY

Some teen-agers, and even adults, pick up anything that isn't fastened down and laugh about it in front of their buddies.   Such a person is insecure and is trying to build his or her ego by showing off.   Buddies who laugh about stealing are not really friends, or they would make their disapproval known.

Before the world became civilized, might was right.   The strong preyed on the weak.   The strong were not necessarily happier as a result of their ill-gotten possessions.   They feared their violent associates and were feared by honest people.

Many times the weak gathered into groups and killed the criminals.   Laws were passed to protect the weak, and police forces were established to enforce the laws so people could live happier and more peaceful lives.

There is a growing tendency in modern, "civilized" society to ignore laws and to consider it a challenge to violate or circumvent them.   Some people do not personally violate laws, but ridicule police and do not cooperate in enforcing laws. They classify as stupid those people who turn in large sums of money found on the street.

In today's society, some lawyers and juries are responsible for excessive awards to people who file injury claims in the courts.   The juries apparently think of themselves as being akin to Robin Hood, i.e., taking money from the rich insurance companies and giving millions of dollars in excess of actual damages to injured citizens.

This forces insurance companies to increase premiums to stay solvent.   This harms everyone.   It harms you because it forces your parents to pay higher auto insurance premiums--possibly so high they cannot afford to let you drive.

Expectant parents also pay a high price because excessive awards in malpractice lawsuits have sent doctor's insurance costs soaring. Some physicians have stopped delivering babies, so there's also a shortage of qualified doctors.

Some neighborhoods are turned into slums because tenants don't properly care for rental property. The tenants contend that the landlords are gouging them and the landlords argue that the tenants won't care for the property, so it's a waste of money to make repairs. The irresponsibility of tenants thus leads to higher rents and substandard living conditions.

Once an antisocial attitude is developed and a prison record established, reform is almost impossible. A few do reform, but the realities of life make it more difficult.

People who violate the law seldom are caught the first time. However, they repeat the offenses until, eventually, they are caught and punished.

They think they are clever because they got away with earlier offenses and received a relatively light penalty for what the court thought was a first offense. The criminals blame getting caught on bad luck or on someone else. It is never their fault. This encourages them to continue, and to increase the seriousness of their offenses until they are in serious trouble.

If offenders do not realize after the first offense or two that they are headed down the wrong path, their bad attitudes will follow them for the rest of their lives. An offender will frequently lose jobs because the boss fires him or her for stealing or learns of the criminal record.

Such people cheat on mates, employers, and the government. They are not trusted by parents, friends or neighbors. They seldom succeed at anything honorable. Many start buying, using and selling drugs because, with a prison record, they have difficulty finding legitimate opportunities. This, in turn, leads to even greater problems.

Here's a story to illustrate how easy it is to start on a downhill slide into a life of problems.

Anne and Lucy were good friends and always together. One day, they were hanging around a shopping center and noticed a display of earrings on the counter. There were several that the girls liked, but they knew their parents would not allow them to buy or charge them.

Lucy took Anne off to the side and suggested they each steal a pair. Anne was horrified at the suggestion and expressed her reservations. Lucy eventually talked her into distracting the sales clerk with questions at the other end of the counter, while Lucy picked up two pairs of earrings and put them in her purse. They weren't caught and giggled over how easy it had been. Lucy suggested they each tell their parents that the other girl's mother didn't like the earrings and gave them to her. It worked.

A pattern of shoplifting was established that continued until they were caught. They were given probation for their "first offense," but now their parents knew they had been stealing. Anne's parents made her earn the money to pay for the stolen item and insisted she drop Lucy as a friend. Word leaked out to their classmates. Anne was embarrassed and decided never again to steal. Lucy bragged about how easy it had been and how easily they had gotten off.

Lucy's parents told her that she was no good and had embarrassed them. They showed no compassion and made Lucy feel she couldn't do anything to please them. She continued her antisocial activities, partly to spite her parents and partly because she thought it was fun to get away with the thefts.

Lucy started associating with a rough bunch of boys and eventually got into drugs. She later dropped out of school and found a job in a factory. She didn't keep it long because she was constantly sneaking out for a cigarette and displaying an unsatisfactory attitude toward her supervisors. The trend continued downward.

Several years later, Lucy was involved in an auto accident caused by a drunken boyfriend who was driving. She died en route to the hospital.

The principle here is: *HONESTY IS ALWAYS THE BEST POLICY.*

There is no way a person can lie, cheat or steal without it seriously affecting his or her future success and happiness. Once a pattern of dishonesty is established, it is almost impossible to break. It is the ATTITUDE that causes the problem, not a single act or series of acts.

FOUL LANGUAGE

In some schools, both boys and girls use foul language. Some of this they get from friends, the movies and, in some cases, from home. They justify use of such language by saying it is the way all the other kids talk. They also may feel it is adult talk and more grown up.

To use such language, particularly sexual words, cheapens the individual in the eyes of responsible people. When a girl uses it, she can be telling a boy she is worldly wise and ready to be "laid." When a boy uses it, he can be saying, "I'm on the prowl for sexual gratification. How about it?"

The people who use such language may deny that they are soliciting sex, but, regardless, the person hearing this kind of language will interpret it his or her way.

Foul language will not be tolerated in most work environments. Many sexual harassment cases are brought by women against men who make suggestive remarks. Such talk can limit opportunities for promotion. If you use foul language, now is the time to get your act together.

A principle here is: *A HANDSOME OR PRETTY FACE IS MADE UGLY BY A FOUL MOUTH.*

DRUGS

Drug dependence is a form of hell on earth. You probably have seen enough with other young people and on TV to know the hazards of drug use, but you may not be fully aware of how easy it is to get "hooked."

There frequently are pushers at teen-age parties in big cities and in many smaller towns. Teens have fun when they act silly. If friends try drugs and start giggling and cutting up, you want to try whatever they are taking. It takes very little coaxing to get a young person started.

Drug peddlers try to convince young people that drugs will give them a wonderful feeling and that they won't become addicted by trying it once. They may even offer the first one free. If you don't have enough self-discipline to say "No" then, you may be headed for real misery.

If you have tried drugs and not become addicted, you are one of the few lucky ones. Once a person starts using drugs, it becomes harder to say, "No," and easier to try more potent drugs. The temporary high a person gets from trying drugs is a giant step toward the gutter and misery.

Marijuana smokers don't have hangovers of any consequence. Marijuana is probably the least addictive drug, but it destroys brain cells that never recover, causes birth defects in children, and has other highly undesirable side effects. Long-time users have poor memories and find it difficult to keep organized.

A drug high can cause misery in the form of jumpy nerves, hangovers, and even loss of self-worth. Everything that goes up must come down. Pilots who take planes into the wild blue yonder come down for smooth landings. The drug user, by contrast, may come down for a crash landing from which he may never recover.

All drugs, crack cocaine in particular, have been disastrous for young people. They can:

(1) Destroy peace and happiness by bringing misery when the "high" wears off;

(2) Turn users into criminals since it takes a great deal of money to satisfy an ever-increasing appetite;

(3) Cause death from (a) overdose, (b) execution by peddlers who don't get paid promptly or whose territories are violated, and (c) AIDS contracted from needles;

(4) Cause an explosive increase in birth defects, child abuse, and parental neglect; and

(5) Destroy not only the users' lives, but also neighborhoods through murder and violence.

Teens in drug rehabilitation tell stories of hopelessness. They are starved for food and affection, are severely underweight and are suspicious human beings.

More simply stated: Use of drugs in any form will most likely ruin your life and impair the happiness of those you love and depend upon most.

If you want to know more about drugs, there is a booklet by Abigail Van Buren (Dear Abby) entitled "What Every Teen Should Know" that describes them and their effect on the body in some detail. Her address is in the back of this book.

A principle to remember is: **DON'T BE MUGGED BY DRUGS.**

SMOKING

Smoking tobacco is something you may have already started. It may be too late for you to quit easily, but the following from a lady who became addicted when she was sixteen may be helpful.

"I was 16 when I was first offered a cigarette by a friend. I didn't particularly like it, but it made me feel more independent and more a part of the crowd. Later I bought a pack and found that the second one wasn't so bad. I finished the pack over a three day period.

"How was I to know that 30 years later I'd be so hooked that any thought of quitting was out of the question. I wake up each morning with a foul taste in my mouth. My teeth are stained and my chest and lungs feel like they are so filled with mucous I can hardly breathe. The thought of not having a cigarette the first thing in the morning, if I run out at night, drives me crazy until I get to the store for a pack. I am constantly lighting up.

"There are burns on all of my nice furniture. One time, I fell asleep with a cigarette in my hand. Fortunately, it burned my hand and woke me up before it caught the bed on fire and burned the house down.

"My dad died of lung cancer. For many years, he had emphysema and had trouble breathing. He also had heart trouble and poor circulation which the doctor says were caused by smoking. I know I am headed down the same miserable path.

"I can't roll back the clock to when I was sweet 16 and had never smoked. I wish to God someone had made me realize then what I know now, that I would become a slave to a filthy and health-destroying habit."

A principle to remember is: *CIGARETTES ARE THE CALM BEFORE A STORM OF DEPENDENCY AND ILL EFFECTS.*

ALCOHOL AND AUTOMOBILES

Alcohol, taken in small quantities, can be beneficial to adults. It is considered a social lubricant. No party is complete without it. Some adults can control drinking and have one or two weak drinks before the evening meal. Some doctors say this releases stress and improves longevity for executives and others in people-oriented situations. Many Europeans drink a glass of wine with almost every meal without apparent harm.

The problem is few people can control their drinking. One drink relaxes inhibitions, so people want a second and a third. Even if you develop self-discipline as suggested in Chapter III, most teen-agers aren't mature enough to control alcohol consumption. It also has many negative effects on the body, particularly in girls.

The effects of alcohol are very different on youths than on adults. Many hormonal changes take place in the body as it matures. Alcohol can cause the maturity process to slow or even stop, and the fluctuation of hormones in the female's monthly cycle makes it more difficult to judge the degree of intoxication.

It is better to avoid alcoholic beverages until you are an adult. Even then, you probably will be happier and more successful in life if you never start drinking.

Many teen-age boys feel they are showing their manhood if they drink a six-pack of beer. This is not only dangerous for a car driver and all passengers, but is also the start of an alcoholic pattern that can cause many problems in later life, the least of which will be a "beer belly."

MADD (Mothers Against Drunk Driving) circulates the following story that graphically presents the hazards of mixing alcohol and automobiles, a deadly mix. The story doesn't mention alcohol, but alcohol seems to increase aggressive behavior and decrease the ability to be sensible. It relaxes both inhibitions and mental control. This relaxation increases with every sip.

Here's a tale that will make anyone think:

"PLEASE GOD, I'M ONLY 17

"The day I died was an ordinary school day. How I wish I had taken the bus! But I was too cool for the bus. I remember how I wheedled the car out of Mom. 'Special favor,' I pleaded. 'All the kids drive.' When the 2:50 bell rang, I threw all my books in the locker. I was free until 8:40 tomorrow morning! I ran to the parking lot, excited at the thought of driving a car and being my own boss. Free!

"It doesn't matter how the accident happened. I was goofing off -- going too fast. Taking crazy chances. But I was enjoying my freedom and having fun. The last thing I remembered was passing an old lady who seemed to be going awfully slow. I heard a deafening crash and felt a terrible jolt. Glass and steel flew everywhere. My body seemed to be turning inside out. I heard myself scream.

"Suddenly, I awakened. It was very quiet. A police officer was standing over me. Then I saw a doctor. My body was mangled. I was saturated with blood. Pieces of jagged glass were sticking out all over. Strange that I couldn't feel a thing.

"Hey, don't pull that sheet over my head! I can't be dead, I'm only 17. I've got a date tonight. I'm supposed to grow up and have a wonderful life. I haven't lived yet. I can't be dead.

"Later, I was placed in a drawer. My folks had to identify me. Why did they have to see me like this. Why did I have to look at Mom's eyes when she faced the most terrible ordeal of her life? Dad suddenly looked like an old man. He told the man in charge, 'Yes, he is my son.'

"The funeral was a weird experience. I saw all my relatives and friends walk toward the casket.

They passed by, one by one, and looked at me with the saddest eyes I've ever seen. Some of my buddies were crying. A few of the girls touched my hand and sobbed as they walked by.

"Please—somebody—wake me up! Get me out of here! I can't bear to see my mom and dad so broken up. My grandparents are so racked with grief they can hardly walk. My brother and sisters are like zombies. They move like robots. In a daze, everybody. No one can believe this. And I can't believe it either.

"Please don't bury me! I'm not dead! I have a lot of living to do! I want to laugh and run again. I want to sing and dance. Please don't put me in the ground. I promise if you give me just one more chance, God, I'll be the most careful driver in the whole world. All I want is one more chance!

"Please, God, I'm only 17!"

Many lives have been destroyed and people maimed for life by drivers who drank too much and wouldn't admit they were drunk. An association of emergency nurses known as CARE (Cancel Alcohol Related Emergencies) compiled the following alarming statistics:*

1. Young drivers (ages 16-24) make up 20% of the population, but are involved in more than 45% of all fatal highway crashes;

2. One out of five fatal auto accidents involve teenage drivers;

3. About 2000 teen-agers are killed each year, and more than 40,000 are injured and/or disfigured for life;

4. Approximately 60% of fatally injured teen-age drivers had alcohol in their blood at the time of

Nordberg, M. (1988) *ED Nurses Take A Stand.* Emergency Medical Services 17-8 p. 20 9-88.

the accident and 43% were at or above the legal level of intoxication;

5. Alcohol-related accidents involving teenagers occur three times more frequently at night; and

6. Of 330 children born today, one will die and four will suffer scarring or crippling injuries in an alcohol-related crash before the age of 24.

Alcohol relaxes inhibitions. It causes some people to become more talkative and to repeat themselves. This bores everyone around. Others, particularly men, frequently become belligerent and start fights.

In a domestic situation, the alcoholic may quarrel with a mate and yell at the children. Occasionally, they even abuse family members. Many marriages are destroyed by men and women who became addicted to alcohol and became impossible to live with.

An intoxicated person thinks he or she is in full control of mental faculties, but capability is confused and disoriented, and judgment is faulty. Many alcoholics are brilliant when sober, but become obnoxious on a binge.

Most alcoholics start with a few drinks on the weekend. This builds stress and makes them feel the need to drink more to relax. Soon, they are drinking every night, and, eventually, get up to a pint or more daily.

If a girl is to avoid sexual encounters, she should avoid dating a heavy drinker and avoid drinking herself. A recent survey found that women had one-third more alcohol in their blood after several drinks than a man of the same weight.

The safest course is to avoid alcoholic parties, but if you are going to drink, establish limits and stick to them. If you feel like drinking more, quit and, if possible, find a group of friends who are teetotalers. Some teetotalers go to parties where alcohol is served, take a glass of gingerale, and sip on it all evening.

Principles to remember are:

BETTER A DESIGNATED DRIVER THAN DEAD OR DISABLED

PLEASURE OBTAINED FROM DRUGS, ALCOHOL, OR TOBACCO IS NOT WORTH THE RESULTING MISERY.

Also don't forget a principle previously mentioned:

DARE TO BE A LEADER.

CHAPTER XI

Other Aids To Building a Happy Life

Teen-agers can improve the quality of life by improving their ability to THINK, by being loyal to friends, family, and country, by getting the most value from dollars spent and by utilizing help available through religion. This chapter has several suggestions on these matters.

SHARPENING YOUR MIND

Some great athletes were physically impaired or suffered serious injuries when young. Kristi Yamaguchi, an ice skater who won a gold medal in the 1992 Olympics, was born with both feet turned inward and the toes facing each other. Roger Bannister, the first man ever to run a mile in four minutes, was seriously burned as a youngster. There was doubt that he would ever walk normally.

Many people with physical problems have worked hard to develop their bodies to a championship level. Similar dedication can overcome many learning problems.

Many young people consider themselves dumb and feel they never will be good students. Others have learning disabilities. Most of these persons can overcome their deficiencies if they make the effort. Effort expended and progress made also will do much to increase self-esteem.

Many slow learners became geniuses by not giving up. Thomas Edison, the father of modern research and inventor of the electric light, voice recording, electric generators and electric distribution systems, had a hearing problem that could have been a learning handicap. Instead, he found ways to learn even after he was expelled from school when the teacher lost patience with him.

Albert Einstein, one of history's great mathematicians and developer of the theory of nuclear power, had a learning disability.

Abe Lincoln, one of our great presidents, didn't have a learning disability, but had very little formal education. By exercising his brain through reading and thinking, he became a great lawyer and won many cases before he became president.

If you have a harder time learning than most other young people, it is no reason to quit trying. You just need to use more self-discipline to develop your brain. If you are deficient in one area, such as mathematics, consult your teachers. If the deficiency is general, you can sharpen your thinking ability by sharpening your reading skills.

Reading sharpens the mind in the same manner as running or swimming strengthens the body. If you read a lot, even fiction, you will find it is easier to read and understand your textbooks. Improving your brain power is an investment that will pay off in higher earnings in later years and greater enjoyment of the world around you.

I believe that my extensive reading when in high school, mentioned in Chapter One, sharpened my mind to the point I was able to overcome the handicap of not having a formal college education.

James Mitchener, the famous writer, had a similar early life experience. He read every children's book in his small town library and, like me, read many of the adult classics. His mother was poor and he never knew his father, but he was able to get a formal degree by hard work and with the help of relatives who recognized his intelligence.

When you read something that is well-written and fascinating, look back to see how the author presented the subject. Make notes in a notebook so that you can review them and try to write something yourself that will be equally spell binding.

Work diligently at whatever you do, but intersperse it with some fun, athletic activity, and at least eight hours of sleep. Too much of one activity or too much concentration on achieving can be as bad as too much time spent on having a good time. Frequently, teen-age suicides result from too much pressure to excel without sufficient time to relax.

Education is what you get if you read a lot. Experience is what you get if you don't.

Here is a principle to remember: *READING DEVELOPS BRAIN POWER AS WELL AS KNOWLEDGE.*

LOYALTY

The dictionary defines loyalty as "being faithful in allegiance to one's sovereign or country or true to plighted faith or duty." Loyalty to country is more than saluting the flag. It is accepting responsibility for, and unselfishly serving, your nation or any group to which you belong, such as your sports team, family, and friends.

The need for loyalty arises from the fact that in unity there is strength. One person can accomplish little by himself, but an army can conquer or defend a nation. A team can win more often if its members and supporters are loyal to the group and work together unselfishly.

Loyalty is similar to love in that it is unselfish. Where there is love, there usually will be loyalty and vice versa.

You are fortunate to be living in the greatest nation in the world. It was made great by the fact that every person has a right to be independent and free, except when that freedom interferes with the unity of the nation, the state or the rights of others. We are free to worship as we please, to vote as we please, and to criticize even the president. But when the chips are down, loyalty and love of country bring us together to do what we must as a united unit.

Democracy is frequently criticized as being inefficient. A great deal of time is spent arguing and discussing, instead of accomplishing. However, the final action that results from such discussion is nearly always the will of the majority. When it isn't, it is because some people did not vote or didn't make their opinions known.

Some people criticize our leaders and our form of government because of many incidents of corruption. However, there is corruption under all forms of government because there are always some people who are selfish and want to get rich by any means. The situation is worse in countries where the citizens and media can't act as watchdogs of government and can't speak out against evil.

If we are to survive as a free nation, we have an obligation to protect our freedom by being loyal to our government, by supporting its laws, by voting, by honoring its flag, by bearing arms, if necessary, and by following the elected leadership even when it isn't our will.

Loyalty to a nation takes precedence over loyalty to a political party or to any organization or any individual. In a primary election, the candidates within a political party compete with each other and frequently harshly criticize each other. However, when the general election comes up, they usually give up private desires and opinions to unite in support of the candidate of the party.

This is democracy in action, which makes our nation strong.

There is a limit to loyalty only to the extent that it hurts someone else or the basic group. If a friend does something dishonorable, loyalty doesn't mean covering up for him or her. It does mean standing up for him or her when attacks are unjust even if it means possible harm to you. It also means giving the person the benefit of doubt until the truth is known. Loyalty to a friend should be second only to loyalty to your group.

If and when you get into trouble, as everyone does occasionally, you will appreciate the loyalty of friends who stand behind you and be forever grateful to them.

Loyalty to a girlfriend, boyfriend, or mate, when you marry, will have many rewards in a happy life. All of us have faults, and it is possible to criticize even saints. Imagine how you would feel if someone close to you said something hateful or unpleasant about you, even if true. You would be furious. Therefore, it behooves you to say nice things about people you like and avoid telling tales about people within your group, whether you like them or not.

A person also benefits indirectly from loyalty to local merchants and manufacturers. A person who buys from a local business out of loyalty, even though a foreign product is available for less, may find that some of the dollars kept in the local community will end up in his or her pocket. If he needs help or advice, the local merchant will be quicker to respond.

It isn't possible to trace the dollars in circulation, but it stands to reason that money sent out of the community means fewer dollars available within the community. Money sent out of the country or the local area is not likely to become available again to pay local workers. Neither will it be available to pay taxes to help the persons who lost jobs due to foreign competition. In fact, the shortage of money in the local community could result in more taxes to you because there will be more people in need and fewer dollars to support local government.

Being loyal to family, friends, team and government is good for the conscience. It builds a team spirit, a form of happiness.

Here's a principle to remember: *LOVE YOUR NEIGHBOR AS YOURSELF.*

USING MONEY EFFICIENTLY

Now, let's look at ways to get the most for your money.

It is difficult to save money because wants nearly always exceed the money supply. Advertisers spend billions of dollars to induce us to spend our last nickel.

If you are totally dependent upon your parents, you have no need to save now, but you soon will be working after school, or during the summer, to buy a car, a stereo or other modern convenience, so it's not too early to think about saving and ways to get the most for your money.

Benjamin Franklin said: "A penny saved is a penny earned." It also is said that, "He who has 99 cents income and spends $1.00 will find unhappiness. He who has $1.00 income and spends 99 cents will find happiness."

Every wage earner must have some discretionary income. This means money that can be used for pleasure and unexpected expenses. Without it, there will be no pleasure and much agony. When a person owns an automobile, there will be many such expenses.

How can a person acquire property and meet these expenses? First, from discretionary income, second, from   savings, if any, and finally by incurring debt.

Buying on credit is the customary way of acquiring costly items.   Some items, such as automobiles, usually are purchased on credit. However, first you must have saved enough for a down payment and the initial insurance premium, which, for young people, usually exceeds $1,000 per year.

Later in life, you may want to buy a home for your family, which also requires the use of both savings and credit.   Of course, a family can rent a house, instead of buying one, but the drain on family income is much greater than if a home is purchased.   Buying a home requires an initial investment of about 10% or 15% or $10,000 to $15,000 on a $100,000 house.

To borrow money, a person must have established a good credit record by paying bills promptly.   Some banks and credit companies lend money to a person who has no credit record, if he or she has a good job.   However, borrowing without a credit rating or security usually calls for a high interest rate.   The rate for credit card purchases can be 18% to 22% per year.   The interest rate for an automobile or home is about half as much.

Using credit to purchase small items can substantially decrease discretionary income because of monthly repayments.   Purchases from stores that specialize in credit sales are 20% or more higher than discount stores.   Even the cost of buying with credit cards at discount stores is relatively high because of carrying charges.   Few people pay any more on credit cards than the required minimum, so these carrying charges go on month after month.

Unpleasant though it may be, getting in the habit of saving money and going into debt are very definitely in your future.   Therefore, it behooves you to think about needs as compared to "wants" before you spend.

Let's look at an example: Becky found a job soon after graduating from high school that paid $300 a week. Deductions took $70 of this, her lunches $15, and room and board to her parents $85. Transportation would take $25 per week, so she decided to buy a second hand car instead, which cost her $70 per week, including insurance, gas and oil. This left $60 of discretionary income, which sounded like plenty.

However, she bought $1,000 worth of clothes on a credit card. The credit company convinced her she should buy credit insurance so her parents wouldn't have to pay the bill if she were killed or disabled. The payments on the loan would be just $47 per month or about $11 per week. She felt she could handle this easily.

The interest rate was 18% annually, or $180 per year. The credit insurance was another $1.00 per week, bringing the annual cost of the debt up to $232.00.

Unfortunately, each week Becky found other things she needed, and the car always seemed to require repairs. When she got a raise, she found even more things she wanted or bought on impulse. She, therefore, kept charging items on the card, and the balance stayed around $1,000 for two years. It went up to $1,300 when a friend invited her to be a bridesmaid.

Becky sat down and did some figuring. During the two years, she had spent $464 on interest and insurance. She had nothing to show for the money. The clothes initially purchased were worn out. She had spent another $1,428 for clothes and personal items, had no savings and still owed $1,300.

She could have gotten along nicely with an initial purchase of $250, which she could have paid off in four months and would have cost only $13 in interest.

Here's how the figures compared:

Item	Cost	Alternate	Saved
Initial purchases	$1,000	250	750
Interest 2 years	464	13	451
Other items purch.	1,428	1,428	0
Total Cost	2,892	1,691	1,201

During the two years, she could have deposited in a saving account an amount equal to the payments she had made on the loan. Thus she would:

(1) Have had the $1,428 cash to buy all of the same items she had purchased on credit;

(2) Be free of debt; and

(3) Would have $1,201 in the bank ($750 less spent initially and $451 interest saved). This would be enough to make a down payment on a new car or to make major repairs on the old car.

Becky realized she would be burdened with the debt and carrying charges forever unless she paid them off and started buying on a cash basis. If she continued as she had been, in another three years, the charges would exceed the amount initially borrowed and the debt still would be outstanding.

Becky immediately worked out a budget and found a number of ways to cut expenses so that she could pay off the debt within the next year. She vowed never again to charge on a credit card without making a special effort to pay the full balance within 30 days. If she charged purchases and paid in full in the following month, there would be no carrying charge and she would establish a good credit record.

She also resolved that after the debt was paid off she would start saving 10% of her income, plus all income tax refunds, so she could pay cash for big expenditures. No longer would she buy impulsively without carefully considering how and when she would pay.

RELIGION

I have urged you to take charge of your life. However, sometimes life's problems become too complex for you to handle alone. Many times your parents can help. At other times, seeking Divine guidance can be very consoling and helpful.

We will assume that you recognize the fact that there is a supreme being. All of us, when we pledge allegiance to the flag, acknowledge that we are one nation under God, with liberty and justice for all.

We will address the evidence that there is a God, as seen by both Christians and Jews, and the practical aspects of religion without going into theological aspects that vary between religions.

Is There a God?

Many people refuse to believe there is a supreme being because they can't see him or feel his presence. Others can't reconcile stories in the Old Testament of the Bible with facts revealed by scientists.

Perhaps God created the world in seven days eons ago, but isn't it more probable that this and many tales in the Old Testament were invented by people to explain things they didn't understand?

Memories are not totally reliable, so each time a story was told, it may have changed slightly. We are always seeking the truth about many things, so why wouldn't people tend to believe tales carried down over the ages if they seemed logical?

After man learned to write on stone tablets, papyrus, or paper, facts could be recorded, and it was no longer necessary to invent tales.

Both Moses and Jesus Christ lived during historical times. We have as much reason to believe these men lived as we do that Napoleon, Caesar or Ghengis Khan lived. Jewish people accept the fact that Jesus Christ lived, but not that he was the Messiah promised by God. It is not necessary to believe that Christ was the Son of God or that he was the Messiah to profit from his teachings. He taught many of the same truths taught by the prophets before him, but in greater detail.

Some say that if there was a God, he would not permit evil in the world. Let's assume that you are God and you give your people freedom to run their own lives. Isn't it logical that some will use the freedom wisely to improve life for themselves and to help others, while some will abuse the privilege by stealing, killing, and committing other crimes for selfish reasons? If there were no freedom to use our brains and to make choices, there could be no happiness. God or some other force would have to direct us every minute of the day and night.

As God, would you ignore the evildoers, or would you try to teach them to be considerate of their fellow men? Obviously, the latter. But how? If God communicated directly with people, would they listen any better than they would to others of their own kind? Probably not. Wouldn't you, as a young person, rather listen to young people your age than to parents, teachers or officials?

Wouldn't it be logical for God to make men on earth his representatives and inspire them to teach people how to respect one another's rights? That's what God did when he sent the prophets and a man who said he was his Son to talk to people and lead them. To get people to listen, he gave his representatives power to part the Red Sea, to heal the blind and the lame, and to bring dead people back to life.

So why not: (1) Accept that there may be some fallacies in the Old Testament invented by men to explain the unexplainable, and (2) Accept truths later revealed through men who obviously had Divine help?

Advantages of Belonging to a Religious Group:

Although churches are religious institutions established for the purpose of worshiping a supreme being, they also benefit the community through good works and bring spiritual comfort to their members.

Most church-going people are warm, kind, and friendly. People who regularly attend church welcome newcomers. They care about others and are less selfish with what they have. They help homes for unwed mothers and people who are terminally ill. They volunteer at the hospitals to care for the ill, and operate facilities for the homeless, battered women, etc.

You may feel that religious people are too "goody, goody" and no fun. How do you know until you have met and joined in their fun? You'll probably have a happier life if you look for a mate among church members. It is the surest way to find a life partner who will be pleasant and loyal to you.

Here's a principle to remember: *FAMILIES THAT PRAY TOGETHER STAY TOGETHER.*

God's representatives on earth are His ministers and rabbis. They are usually trained in counseling and have experience helping and advising troubled people. The Bible and other books that contains God's teachings reflect the wisdom of great minds over the ages.

At times, you may have problems that trouble you greatly. If your conscience bothers you about wrongs you have committed, you can find peace by talking to a minister or religious leader. What you say will be kept absolutely confidential, unless you agree that your parents should be brought into the discussion.

You also have school counselors you can talk to, but you may want to keep the problem from school officials. If something is troubling you to the point you're losing sleep, find an adult somewhere who will listen to you and ask him or her to advise you.

When you get ready to marry, it will be wise to consult with a disinterested and trained counselor, such as a clergyman, about your selection of a mate. If you fall madly in love (infatuation?), you may feel that you do not want to listen to anyone, but MARRIAGE IS (or should be) A LIFETIME COMMITMENT and worthy of careful consideration.

It is much easier to break an engagement than a marriage. Broken hearts heal surprisingly fast when there is no property or children to consider, so get another opinion from a qualified person.

Of course, if you are going to feel free to consult a minister, you should be reasonably active in a church. Most ministers will help anyone who asks for it, but, if they have known the person seeking help for some time, they will be more relaxed and better able to give sound advice.

How Does God Reward Good People and Punish Evildoers?

The Bible teaches that we will be rewarded or punished after death for good and bad deeds. However, many of the rewards and punishment can occur while we are still on earth.

God works through the subconscious mind and prayer. He may or may not answer prayers to our satisfaction, but, frequently, when we lay a problem before Him, the answer comes to us in the middle of the night or the next time we consider the matter. Some call it incubation, but you have to be relaxed for it to work.

When we put the matter in His hands, we suddenly feel calmer and not so much alone. By praying, we gain inner strengths that we didn't know we had. These strengths help us solve our problems and live a happier life.

Prayer also may help others. A study was made to determine if the above statement is true. A report, written by Dr. Randolph C. Byrd and published in the July 1988 Southern Medical Journal, examined the effect of prayer on the recovery rate of 393 patients admitted to the Coronary Care Unit at San Francisco General Hospital.

The patients were divided into two groups of equal size. Those in the first group would receive the benefit of prayers while those in the second, called a "control" group, would not.

Prayer persons were selected from members of several Protestant and Roman Catholic churches. Each patient in the prayer group was assigned to three to seven prayer persons who knew only the first names and general condition of their subjects, but did not know them personally. Prayer persons were asked to pray for rapid recovery and prevention of complications.

Twenty-seven of the prayer group patients died or suffered reversals as opposed to forty-four of the control group. Two of the prayer group patients showed no significant improvement, as opposed to ten of the control group.

Of the prayer group patients, 163 had substantially improved heart conditions, as compared with 147 in the control group, a difference of 16 patients.

Some of us will die through accidents, but, sooner or later, we must leave this world to make room for new life. Don't expect a miracle. Although miracles can occur through faith healing and simple prayer, they are rare. It is expecting too much to expect God to intercede in the living and dying process. It is up to each of us to take proper care of ourselves.

Steve Bartowski, a former pro football star, looking back on his playing days, said:

"With all my wealth, I was never satisfied. I felt empty inside. I couldn't understand why I wasn't the happiest person in the world. I would stay out all hours drinking and partying, and I didn't have any problem gaining the company of attractive young ladies. But during those nights, it seemed like the emptiness I had inside deepened."

His performance on the football field during this period deteriorated, and his wife divorced him. He joined a church and his life changed. His football performance also improved.

"I felt a great peace about the situation I was in, even though at that moment my circumstances hadn't changed at all," he said. "I seemed to have a new perspective on life, and my problems didn't seem quite as drastic. My attitude toward people changed. Jesus taught me to love others and to care for them."

This young man probably would have made a similar statement if he had joined any faith. He might have used God in his statement instead of Christ.

Excuses For Not Attending Services:

A good way to prevent being bored by religious services is to participate. Most sermons seem to apply to adults and usually include theological rhetoric that is hard to follow. If you participate in the singing and praying and try to interpret sermons into everyday language, you will find it less boring. Socializing afterward with other young people or joining a youth activity also will help.

Some adults, and probably many young people. say they don't go to church because hypocrites go to church or because some TV evangelists don't practice what they preach. There are many selfish people in the world who misuse their power and God-given talents, but that doesn't mean we have to follow in their footsteps.

In church, you will find a hundred kind and unselfish people for every hypocrite. You will find a thousand ministers who practice their religion for every one who exploits it.

ACTION SECTION

(1) On your Take Charge list, enter several books you will read in the near future. Give a starting date and place for locating the book.

(2) Tell your parents you want some experience handling money and would like a clothing allowance. If they have a charge account, they won't need to give you cash, but you must keep track of the amount spent and stay within the budget limit.

Also suggest that you be given an allowance large enough to cover incidentals. This will constitute discretionary income. Then, ask them if they will add half of the savings on clothes to this allowance so you can save money for special items. If, at the end of the period, you still have some allowance left, perhaps your parents will add half of it to your discretionary income rather than have you spend all of it.

Use a note book to keep track of both allowances. Be careful not to spend all of either allowance at one time. If the clothing allowance is for a quarter or a whole year, divide the amount over the period and don't make any purchases until the accumulated allowance will cover expenditures. This will give you the feeling of having a steady income you can save until you have a real need rather than a "want."

If you don't keep within your allowance, you can expect your parents to revoke the privilege and, possibly, comment about irresponsibility. If you keep proper records and keep within the allowance, it will show that you are trustworthy and responsible, and you will, undoubtedly, be given more freedom to make your own decisions in the future.

(3) If you haven't attended a religious service lately, make a written commitment to yourself to attend services or Sunday school on three dates within the near future. If you have a friend you know who already attends services, call him or her and ask for recommendations on youth programs.

CHAPTER XII

Understanding Behavior

The early teens is the ideal time to start planning for a happy and fulfilling future. If you wait until tomorrow, next month or next year, many of the good things in life will pass you by.

In this chapter we will discuss **behavior patterns** and how to use them to: (1) choose a career you will like, and (2) motivate others to do things you want done. They also can be used to determine the compatibility of a future mate.

BEHAVIOR PATTERNS

Where strong emotions, such as love, anger and fear are involved, everyone reacts in a similar fashion. However, where values, such as knowledge and judgment, are involved, there is a wide variance in behavior. It is possible to classify this variable behavior into four broad categories or types of behavior. These are (1) dominance, (2) interpersonal relations, (3) stability and (4) compliance. Some values, such as reliability and honesty, and traits, such as optimism, influence behavior within these four classifications.

The titles for the classifications are general terms and should not be taken as absolute descriptions. For convenience, the letters D, I, S, and C will frequently be used in lieu of the full title of each classification.

Each classifications is subdivided into levels which are numbered from 10 to 1. Everyone's behavior fits within each of the four classifications at some level. A person's behavior can be summarized simply by using the letter designation for a classification, followed by the number for the appropriate level. Thus, we can state a behavior pattern as being: "8D,5I,2S,5C."

Note that the numbers in the above pattern cross total to 20, indicating an average of 5 for the four classifications. This illustrates how behavior patterns usually balance out, with some high, some low, but average over all. Most people have one or more strong behavior characteristics, and very few are level 5 in all four classifications.

Descriptive words, as well as numbers, are used to describe the high and low end of each classification. For example, the words aggressive and agreeable are used for the high and low ends of the DOMINANT or D classification.

It is important that you understand that reference to the low end of a classification doesn't imply a negative any more than a low note in a musical scale implies a negative. For example, the low end of the DOMINANT classification (agreeability) means the person avoids conflict. It is a behavior that we want our friends to have and we would like to have, provided we could prevent others from taking undue advantage of us.

There are both favorable and unfavorable aspects of the highs and lows in each of the four behavior classifications. No one is perfect, and there are always offsets to the good and bad things in life. Acceptance of each person's uniqueness also will make it easier for you to work with, be friends with, live with, and be happy with other people without trying to change their natural behavior.

Dominance

High D (DOMINANT) people are aggressive and like to have power and to take charge. As used here, the term "aggressive" means strongly motivated, not quarrelsome or hostile.

High D people evaluate situations quickly and act promptly. They are assertive, authoritative, competitive in sports and social situations, and focus on logic and facts. They like to organize and get the job done. They are not worriers and tend to be insensitive to others.

Low D (AGREEABLE) people are considerate of other people's feelings and usually reluctant to take command. Getting along with others and being of service is vital to their sense of well-being. They tend to react emotionally to the insensitive attitude of an aggressive person, but usually respond diplomatically.

A person who would rate 5 on DOMINANCE would be glad or willing to take charge if given authority, but would not seek or assume authority without authorization. He or she would be considerate of the feelings and wishes of both subordinates and superiors, would be dominant enough to take corrective action when warranted, and would resist unauthorized authority.

Level 5 in other classifications will not be discussed hereafter because it will be assumed you can reasonably determine behavior half-way between high and low levels.

Interpersonal Relations

The second classification is INTERPERSONAL RELATIONS. The person at the high end of the I classification is an EXTROVERT or highly sociable person. The person at the low end is an INTROVERT.

EXTROVERTS are very interested in people and in actions going on around them. They are outgoing and get along well with almost everyone. They tend to be impulsive, rather than deep thinkers. Intelligent extroverts get what they want by flattery and persuasion, rather than by ordering or demanding.   If also high D (DOMINANT), they won't take "No" for an answer.

INTROVERTS are preoccupied with their own thoughts, words, and emotions.   They like to work alone or with a limited number of very close friends.   They like scientific subjects, mathematics and working with things, rather than people.   They aren't very talkative and seldom laugh out loud.

Introverts are more self–conscious than extroverts.   They tend to think carefully before speaking and may be shy.   They will speak up if adequately motivated.   They find it more difficult to make friends than extroverts.   They are usually friendly if the other person starts the conversation.

Stability

The third classification is STABILITY.   The words stable, sensitive and steady best describe the high end of this classification.   The person at the low end of the STABILITY classification is VERSATILE.

High S (STABLE) people like to follow a pattern of living and doing things.   They are sensitive, caring people and are easily upset.   They don't like to take risks and are conservative.   They like to work systematically and steadily to bring work projects to a conclusion.   They are relaxed doing routine and repetitive work and are averse to change.   They like to save things, thinking they'll come in handy some day.

Low S (VERSATILE) people are restless and like variety.   They dislike detail and sedentary work.   They are explorers and use imagination and intuition to find new and better ways to do things. They aren't particularly sensitive because they are on the move.

Low S people can be just as dependable as high S people, so don't let the STABILITY label mislead you.   These people just like more variety in

activities.   Dependability   is   a   matter   of   values
(integrity and self-discipline).

Compliance

The fourth classification is COMPLIANCE.   The
words COMPLIANT and NON-COMPLIANT best describe
the high and low end of this classification.

High C (COMPLIANT)   people follow the rules
and precedents.   They complete what they start and
are neat and clean.   They like to live by a schedule, but can be versatile within the structure of
precedents, rules and laws.

Low C (NON-COMPLIANT) people want FREE-
DOM from restraint.   They deal easily with unexpected happenings and last minute changes in
plans.   They start projects easily when motivated,
but have difficulty finishing them.   This is because
they don't like to be pinned down and because
something else comes up that interests them more.
They have difficulty making up their minds because
they don't want to miss any options.   They tend to
make impulsive decisions they may later regret.

These people who want freedom from restriction are the rebels and frequently in trouble at
school or with the law.   A low C may skip school or
come home late when he or she is having fun.   Such
a person is compulsive, gets upset easily and makes
a big fuss over rules he or she thinks are unfair.
They are usually quick to argue and may be considered stubborn.

Goals, schedules, and commitments are avoided
by Low C's.   This becomes a virtue in an emergency.   They forget schedules and commitments and
do what is needed to remedy situations.   They
willingly break rules and precedents and often fail
to use caution if they see a reason to take risks.
They don't worry about risk if a person is
drowning.

The low end of the COMPLIANT classification
doesn't necessarily include the student who wants

to be able to make decisions free from parental restrictions. Every teenager wants that.

It may seem that the STABILITY and COMPLIANCE classifications are so similar they shouldn't be separated. For example, both STABLE and COMPLIANT persons comply with the rules and regulations. The difference is apparent, however, in the case of a law officer who likes his work. A High C officer follows the rules willingly, but would get bored with a job that didn't have new and different situations every day. Since High S people are sensitive to people and their emotions, they find dealing with criminals stressful. Therefore, it takes a Low S person to enjoy police work.

MODIFIED BEHAVIOR

A person will alter relaxed or natural behavior according to the needs of a particular situation. The resulting behavior then becomes apparent behavior.

For example, if acquiring wealth is important to a person (a part the person's value system), he or she will be more aggressive in a situation involving money. A teacher who is below average in DOMINANCE will be aggressive with students he or she must control.

A normally agreeable person, whose parents taught him or her to stand up for personal rights, will become stubborn and aggressive when those rights are being violated.

A young person who has been mistreated by adults will tend to be rebellious and low on COMPLIANCE. Such a person can become more compliant if and when he or she realizes that a rebellious attitude has been creating more trouble than benefit.

Occasionally, a Low C person will change his or her usual behavior to suit a lover, but don't count on it. A Low C will be quicker to promise than to abide by those promises.

There are courses taught by consultants and industrial psychologists that help people who are weak in certain areas to modify behavior to fit a particular need. However, like a spring that is stretched, these individuals return to their usual behavior patterns in a relaxed situation.

BEHAVIOR VARIATION BY SEX

Dr. Janet Hyde* reviewed a number of studies on gender differences. Information, shown in parentheses here, is explanatory and not from the report:

1. There is no proof that women are less intelligent than men. Their IQ's are approximately equal. Women are better students in school and just as capable in mathematics. As they grow older, they become more interested in social and human-istic subjects, and men become more interested in mathematics and science.

2. Although men in general are more ag-gressive (High D) than women, the difference is much less than usually perceived.

3. Females are somewhat easier to influence (Low D) than males and somewhat more conforming (High C), but the difference is small.

4. Some studies show girls are more fearful, timid and anxious than boys (High S), but other studies show no difference. (The nurturing instinct would seem to make women more security conscious, which is High S behavior.)

* Hyde, J. S. (1985). *Half The Human Experience: The Psychology of Women* (3rd Ed.). Lexington, Mass., D. C. Heath & Co.

5. Evidence does not support the notion that females are more social than males. (This statement seems to contradict the fact that women usually outnumber men at church and social affairs.) While boys tend to congregate in large groups or gangs, girls are more likely to interact in pairs or small groups.

(6) There is no difference in measurable values such as honesty, conscientiousness, and sincerity.

Gender behavior differences have nothing to do with superiority or inferiority. Both men and women have important and overlapping roles in the affairs of the world and have equal rights under law.

HOW BEHAVIOR TYPES INTERACT

The four behavior types fit together so that no person is likely to be high in all four or low in all four. If a person is high in one classification, he or she will be low in another. For example, the highly aggressive person, figuratively speaking, will tend to step on toes, which is low COMPLIANCE. This person is not likely to be sensitive and, since he or she likes to take charge, will want to try new things, making him or her versatile (Low S), and near the middle, or slightly below, in INTERPERSONAL RELATIONS.

A difference in just one classification may substantially change a person's behavior. For example, a woman who is Low D (agreeable) and High S (stable) should be an excellent mother. She is likely to control the children through love and understanding, rather than strong discipline.

High D (aggressive) and Low S (versatile) women love their children just as much, but they want either careers or involvement outside the home. Those with appropriate education and experience make good executives. They expect more from their children and are stricter.

My behavior pattern is 5D,2I,6S,7C. Here's what those four letters and four digits tell you about my personality.

The 2I indicates that I am an introvert and more logical than emotional. I still have emotions and concern for others, but my feelings aren't as strong as they would be in an extrovert. The 7S indicates stability and sensitivity. When the 2I is related to 5D and 6C, it indicates that I like to do and bring projects involving things or logic to conclusion, such as this book. The 5D indicates an average aggressiveness to overcome obstacles and to take charge.

CHOOSING A CAREER

Once a famous professional golfer made a spectacular shot under a tree limb, over a pond, and onto the green. A bystander commented about what a lucky shot it was. The pro heard it, laughed and said, "You know, the more I practice, the luckier I get." Because he prepared for the future, he prepared for success. It didn't just happen.

The best coaches say that the teams that win are those who are prepared to take advantage of good breaks when they occur. If you have already decided upon a career path based upon your strengths, you are indeed wiser than most.

Most schools have tests that analyze skills, likes and dislikes and recommend suitable occupations. Usually the student is told he or she would do well in certain fields, but not the facts that led to that recommendation. Hence, he or she may not value the recommendation highly.

The purpose of this section is to emphasize why you should follow such recommendations and to suggest acceptable alternatives if you disagree.

Many people take up occupations they *enjoy* without knowing what motivated them in that direction. In such cases it is not important to know why they like the work.

Many study for professions based on expectation of high earnings, or take jobs at the urging of parents, without regard to how those jobs fit their personalities. Frequently, the result is unhappiness and low productivity.

Well-balanced people plan careers in work that utilizes their strong points. They seek a well-rounded education, but concentrate on the subjects that fit their natural behavior patterns. For example, the extrovert can develop friendships and prepare for a people-oriented career rather than a technically oriented one. They might be content with being average in math and science and specialize in literary and social subjects that will be useful in law, teaching, sales, social work or other people-related fields.

Here is a principle to remember: "ALL GOOD STRUCTURES START WITH A GOOD PLAN." This applies to building a good life as well as constructing a building. Also remember: "NO SWEAT, NO GAIN."

Individuals who are High D and C and low I and S make good Army or police officers. They dominate situations and don't care if subordinates or criminals like them. An officer with an average I or C would be more popular, however.

Low D, High I and High S (Agreeable, extroverted, and sensitive) people make good teachers and ministers because they are sensitive and interrelate well with others. They also can become good actors because they can turn their emotions off and on much easier than introverts.

Extroverts with average DOMINANCE make good sales persons. If they also are versatile (Low S) and average or above on COMPLIANCE, they make good managers. Good managers are usually average or above on C because they must follow legal and accounting rules in business. They can't be impulsive (low C) because errors are costly.

Introverts are happier and more productive doing work in accounting, construction, engineering, and mechanical jobs. They also do well as writers and reporters where accuracy and dedication to an objective are required.

Introverts can become good salesmen, especially in technical areas where they can plan presentations and take repeat orders. They wouldn't like sales jobs where it is necessary to hunt for customers and meet new people every day.

Introverted doctors are likely to be good diagnosticians but brusque with patients. They are thinking about details of the illness and medication, rather than how patients react. However, extroverted doctors have better doctor-patient relationships.

People high on stability like and do well in clerical and blue collar jobs. Those with good educations make good lawyers and professors. They learn to do complex jobs and are content to do quality work. They can be aggressive or agreeable, depending on the work. If they meet the public, they will be more at ease if they are at least average extroverts.

During my business career, I was active in several trade associations and occasionally worked with many large company presidents. Without exception, they were warm friendly people. They were very knowledgeable, but didn't seem smarter than other company officers. A typical pattern was average on DOMINANCE (D5) and above average on INTERPERSONAL RELATIONS (I7 or I8).

They knew how to get along with and supervise others without creating unnecessary friction. In every organization, there are usually several officers who are High D's and very capable in their particular specialties. However, they have powerful egos that, at times, cause conflict. The president, through careful and friendly handling, keeps them working together with a minimum of friction.

It is interesting to note that many women have behavior patterns that are consistent with those found in chief executives. It follows that women who have this management behavior pattern, reasonable versatility and the necessary business knowledge, would be good managers.

USING BEHAVIOR PATTERNS TO MOTIVATE

Many times you want someone to do something for you or with you, especially family members and friends. Here are some examples of using behavior patterns to motivate people.

Everyone responds well to flattery and appreciation. Nearly everyone also responds to emotional appeals, such as love, pride and loyalty to family, team, country, God, or alma mater. Some even respond to hate and intolerance of other social groups. Most respond to logical and well-planned appeals.

Aggressive people have strong egos, which makes them more susceptible to flattery and more sensitive to criticism. They admire a person who can think for himself or herself, but quarrel with other highly dominant individuals.

To influence a dominant person, plant an idea, get him to ask questions, and let him or her come up with solutions. High D people also respond well to those who are calm and logical.

Usually, dominant children don't get along well with a dominant parent. One young man handled a dominant father who was yelling at him by saying, "Calm down, pappy. The job will get done quicker with a simple request and appropriate instructions." The father was so surprised, he laughed. If the son had reacted by yelling back, it would have made his father more angry.

Agreeable (Low D) people are very polite and react well to simple requests and emotional appeals.

Extroverts (High I) are motivated best by emotion but respond well to logical appeals.

Introverts (Low I) respond better to ideas and logic than to emotional appeals.

Low compliance behavior (low C) people are quick to help friends when there are emergencies. They respond to dares and emotional appeals.

Here is a suggestion as to how to keep class bullies from picking on you. Remember that High Ds have strong egos and want you to be aware of their power. Use flattery. They want to be noticed and will be offended if you ignore them.

Try not to show fear, but talk to them as equals. If the friendly approach doesn't work, try verbal aggression. Speaking up will work better than running or cringing. People who cringe can expect to be picked on. Those who stay calm and try to avoid trouble will usually succeed.

ACTION SECTION

(1) On a sheet of paper write the names of two people who seem to you to be high and two who seem to be low in each behavior classification. The purpose is to become conscious of differences in behavior.

(2) If you have found this chapter interesting, chart your own behavior. You will find instructions on how to do this in Appendix C.

CHAPTER XIII

Loving and Mating For Life

It may be many years before you marry. Nearly everyone gets married sooner or later. However, since you will be constantly faced with decisions about love and the effect of current sex activities on your future, it is not too early to think about the type of mate who will make you happy.

Date to have fun. Don't worry about the future until you feel you are falling in love. Then, you will have to rely upon information stored in your brain to decide whether you <u>are</u> in love and compatible enough with another person to live happily together for a lifetime.

Most young people are seeking a perfect mate and a lifetime of "perfect love." That's not realistic since two people will never agree on everything, and no one is perfect. True love, yes. Perfect love, no.

True love, commitment, and compatibility are all necessary for a successful and happy marriage. Commitment refers to keeping promises to forsake all others and to care for each other in sickness and in health. Compatibility refers to capability of living or functioning harmoniously with another person.

One section of this chapter is devoted to compatibility and another to commitment, but first let's look at the practical aspects of marriage as compared with living together arrangements.

MARRIAGE AS A WAY OF LIFE

Under natural law and church laws, the purpose of marriage is to form a family and raise children to adulthood. There are a few people, however, who don't marry because they want to be independent or believe a mate and children will interfere with career responsibilities. There is a strong possibility they will eventually regret the decision to remain single or to enter into a sexually-oriented relationship without real commitment.

Statistics show that married people outlive singles. This may be because couples who have sincerely made a lifetime commitment can depend upon each other for companionship, as well as physical and moral support in times of stress (such as illness or losing a job or a close relative).

You can realize how important this support is by imagining yourself with a high fever, being too sick to go to a doctor, and having no one to advise or physically help you do what you must. Remember: "NO MAN IS AN ISLAND."

Advantages of marriage are: (1) Sex urges are being satisfied, which brings contentment and relaxation; (2) Fulfillment of the need to love and be loved for life; (3) Security through documented confirmation of a lifetime commitment; and (4) A legal basis for sharing property and for giving a child a name.

COMMITMENT

Marriage is not just a piece of paper as some people contend. It is a commitment between two people to make a life together and to stay together "through sickness and health until death." This means: (1) being faithful to the mate; (2) being willing to share and accommodate each other; and (3) finding ways to resolve differences.

Fidelity--Men and women must make a special effort to satisfy the reproductive instincts of their mates. This means the man shows love and affection for his wife by kissing, hugging and considering her wants and needs. She, in turn, recognizes that he may have a greater need for sexual gratification and strives to make herself attractive to him.

Many people recognize a mate's instinctive needs, but withhold favors to punish the other, with disastrous results. Because sexual instincts are so strong, it is easy to drift into extra-marital relationships. Surveys show that more than half of married men and women have, at one time or another, had such relationships.

When a person learns of an affair of a mate, the jealousy and feeling of betrayal are so overwhelming that trust and true love frequently are destroyed. In such a case, children's security and happiness also are shattered.

A married person is entitled to fidelity, sexual relations, and fair treatment from a spouse, but must earn and work to keep love alive. Love is **internal,** and it doesn't exist by demand or command.

Sharing and Accommodating--Happily married people enjoy each other's company, trust each other, share the same interests, don't keep track of who owes whom, and enjoy many of the same things. They accept their differences and make compromises to keep the relationship happy.

When both are employed, each benefits from the better income. Therefore, they should share the housekeeping, child care, and financial decisions. However, each individual should make decisions on sixty percent give and forty percent take. In a fifty-fifty split, each person might tend to undervalue the other's contribution.

Selfish problems are less obvious at the courtship stage than differences in values. When a person is courting, he or she is putting on a good front. To get to really know a person, depend upon observation rather than conversation. Observe how the person treats others.

Selfish attitudes that may indicate lack of true commitment include:
(1) Won't agree to fairly share work load;
(2) Isn't considerate of other people, including relatives;
(3) Seldom says, "I'm Sorry" or "I forgive you;"
(4) Has very few friends;
(5) Unwilling to help those in need;
(6) Doesn't want children; and
(7) Won't discuss financial matters.

Resolving Differences--Differences occur in marriages and must be resolved by compromise or accommodation. This means: (1) Forgiving past transgressions provided the offending party is truly repentant and wants to make amends; (2) Burying hurt pride; and (3) Communicating to find a way to renew the love once felt and to prevent similar problems.

If the cause of problems is (1) jealousy due to infidelity, (2) frequent quarrels, or (3) poor communication, an attempt to resolve the differences through a third party might result in a happier future for both.

There usually is a way to renew the love that once was there. Many churches have "Marriage Encounter" weekends, and there are many professional marriage counselors qualified to help. If one of the parties is abusive, extremely selfish or repeatedly unfaithful, divorce may be the only satisfactory solution.

COMPATIBILITY

If two people are compatible and truly in love, living together in marriage will make their love grow. Conversely, two people whose personalities do not blend well will quarrel constantly, see love die, and, probably, divorce.

A romance with the wrong person may result in a lifetime of regret.   Even though breaking up is hard, it is not as difficult as divorce, especially if there are children.

Courtship is the best time to evaluate your special friend as a lifetime mate.   Don't worry about losing a lover.   You will become infatuated several times before you really fall in love that will last a lifetime.

Compatibility involves many factors.   Three major ones are:

(1) Parity,
(2) Value systems, and
(3) Compatible behavior.

Parity

For a happy marriage, there must be a feeling of parity or equality.   To avoid friction and a feeling of inferiority or superiority, most couples need to be approximately equal on social level, financial contributions to the marriage, and general intelligence.

Parity exists between two young people with similar educations, but it might disappear if one goes on to obtain an advanced college degree.

Contributions to the marriage need not be similar, but must have equal value in the eyes of the mates.   For example, if the husband works and the wife takes care of the home and children, each relies on the other and each makes a valuable contribution.   The same is true if the wife is the working person and the husband takes care of the home.

Value Systems

In a good marriage, value systems of mates are similar on matters relating to their relationship.

Difference of opinions on matters other than relationship, such as politics, cause no problem.

Would you change your opinion about something you think is important, such as your family,
your religion, neatness, or physical fitness to
accommodate a lover. Certainly not. It takes more
than a few words to change an opinion based on
years of learning and experience.

There is a good chance you won't fall in love
with someone with a substantially different value
system. After a few months of dating, you will
grow apart instead of fall in love. However,
physical or sexual attraction may blind two people,
regardless of differences in values.

For example, the muscular football hero may
marry the class beauty without either of them
giving a second thought to how their values and
personalities will merge or clash over the years.
They don't realize that "compatibility" is more
important in a mate than popularity or physical
beauty. The latter are temporary attractions that
may disappear in a few years.

If your proposed mate indicates that your
good looks are especially important to him or her,
be flattered, but look deeper to see if your
intended is *overly* attracted to other pretty and
handsome faces or figures. However, guard against
becoming jealous over normal sexual attraction. If
the attraction is vanity, such as wanting to have an
attractive partner, he or she may fall out of "love"
with you as you age.

Most values are easy to determine in normal
conversation and observation because they are so
meaningful to us. However, some opinions are kept
private for one reason or another. There is no
harm in keeping quiet about past mistakes and
personal history that have no effect on the future.

Differences in the following areas cause
serious conflicts in marriage: (1) family
relationships, including in-laws, (2) religion, (3)

finances, (4) personal cleanliness and neatness, and (5) physical fitness.

Family--Most young people accept family relationships as a part of living, without analyzing what makes a happy family. They seldom realize how important a mate's family will be to their future happiness. As people grow older, the family generally becomes much more important as a source of love and affection.

When you marry, your spouse will treat you the same as he or she does members of his or her family. To evaluate a potential mate, observe how he or she treats his or her relatives. If the relatives are quarrelsome, also observe how your friend treats your relatives.

Religion--When young people feel they are in love, religion seldom seems of consequence. It does make a difference in later years when there is serious illness, deaths, or births. Many people, especially parents, have such strong feelings about their religion that they tend to aggravate religious differences a young couple might have.

Those without strong religious convictions, but who live a moral life can be, and usually are, more flexible on religious matters.

Finances--How money should be budgeted and spent probably causes more divorces than any other value. If one person is a planner and the other spends money first and isn't concerned about paying the bills, there will be major frustration to both, and probably serious quarrels.

You can evaluate financial responsibility by observing how your potential mate handles his or her money.

Neatness and Cleanliness--If one person believes in neatness and cleanliness and the other is slovenly, they are not likely to be attracted to each other. However, if they are otherwise physically or sexually compatible, they might marry, hoping to change the other's lifestyle. Eventually this may cause conflict.

Physical Fitness--If one person works at being physically fit and eats only health foods, while the other eats too much, gains weight or becomes lazy, the physically conscious mate may lose respect, make critical remarks, and even withhold sex privileges.

Compatible Behavior

Behavior patterns are more complex than value systems, but are useful in picking a compatible life partner.

Behavior patterns are somewhat instinctive, but can be altered slightly by experiences or a particular situation. In a marriage, each person will follow his or her relaxed behavior pattern.

It is frequently said that opposites attract. This is generally true within a behavior classification provided each person recognizes the differences and doesn't try to change, but helps, the other.

There is one exception where opposites don't attract. When one mate is COMPLIANT (High C) and the other NON-COMPLIANT (Low C), there may be some friction because the low C will agree to almost anything, but frequently won't abide by the agreement. This will be very frustrating to the COMPLIANT person who keeps promises and follows rules and precedents.

Two people with similar behavior patterns have a good chance at a happy marriage unless both are highly Dominant or both low on Compliance. In the case of two DOMINANT (High D) personalities, each frequently will take charge and try to control the other, resulting in quarrels. Two NON-COMPLIANT (Low C) personalties will also quarrel because each wants freedom from restriction and won't cooperate or communicate with the other to keep peace.

You might be interested to know how behavior patterns meshed in Grandpop's marriage. Remember I told you my behavior pattern was 5D,2I,6S,7C. The 2I says that I am an introvert and I like analyzing and solving problems. The combination of 5D (average DOMINANCE) and 7C (high COMPLIANCE) means that once I work out a problem, I am very sure of the correctness of my answer. Then it is difficult for anyone to change my mind.

My wife is 2D,7I,8S,3C. The 2D (low DOMINANCE) means she is very agreeable and reluctant to take charge. The 7I (EXTROVERT) means she is very sociable and most everyone likes her. (All of the members of her family had the same type of personality. I liked her family and her mother most of all.) It also indicates she dislikes figures and is very definitely not mechanically inclined.

The 8S (high STABILITY) means she is sensitive, dislikes changes, and prefers a stable living pattern. The 3C (moderately low COMPLIANCE) means she is very independent and resists control.

When we were courting, I enjoyed her willingness to do things my way. After a year of going together and one or two attempts on my part to break it off because I wanted freedom, I finally realized I was in love and that I was ready for a permanent relationship. Further, I recognized that I was too serious and that she would help me be more sociable.

How did two such different personalities keep from quarrelling? At first, she gave in to me most of the time, but, finally, she rebelled because she said I was stubborn and never gave in. I told her that I did concede to reasonable requests because I loved her, but, when I knew I was right, I stood my ground.

This discussion made me realize that a person who always tries to be right builds a barrier that most people see as stubborness and lack of willingness to compromise. Thereafter, when she rebelled, I frequently gave in with a kiss and hug even though I felt I was right. I also tried to consult with her more frequently before making decisions.

Sometimes, we had strong differences of opinion that lasted a day or two. However, instead of quarreling and saying something to hurt the other, we showed our displeasure by refusing to talk. When we calmed down, our differences were resolved without further difficulty. This system worked because she was a peace lover and I'm not very talkative. As we grew older, differences were rare.

We had eight children, so money was a problem from the marriage date until our children were grown. But, by planning, determination, imagination, and some luck, we always made ends meet. I handled the finances and she made most of the day-to-day decisions on children.

We have had a happy life. She was a loving mother. Most of our children are achievers, possibly due to my influence, and nice people because of her's. All have college degrees. Three have master's degrees and one a double masters. None have ever been in trouble with the law.

Here is a principal to remember: **MARRIAGES BETWEEN PEOPLE MADLY IN LOVE SELDOM LAST, BUT MARRIAGES BETWEEN PEOPLE QUIETLY IN LOVE LAST FOREVER.**

TRIAL MARRIAGE

A legal marriage entered into by two people with the understanding they will get a divorce if "things don't work out," is, in effect, a trial marriage.

Many couples live together on a trial basis without getting married. They feel that a marriage license is just a piece of paper. If they decide to split and are not legally bound, it is a simple matter to divide their possessions and go their separate ways. This is easier than going through a legal divorce, but still can be heartbreaking to one or both of the partners.

A divorce can be very traumatic, especially if there are children. The involvement of lawyers frequently increases the difficulties, since they rarely suggest trying to solve problems through compromise. Lawyers are not marriage counselors. Their only obligations are to protect property rights and to get custody of children for their clients, which nearly always causes conflict.

Many men will sleep with any woman who is willing and available, and some women will accept almost any man. If a person is not willing to make a lifetime commitment, it is logical to assume that he or she wants the relationship primarily to satisfy sexual appetite. Some males also want a servant, and some females want companionship and financial security.

If a man and woman join into a sex-oriented partnership and the man is free to leave, there is a good chance that he will do so if his current girlfriend becomes pregnant or if he finds another woman who makes him feel he is a desirable and wonderful man. A woman might feel free to leave for similar reasons.

A word of caution about falling in love with a married man or woman. A person involved with a married man or woman cannot reasonably expect the paramour to leave his or her spouse, especially if there are children.

Other problems: (1) A person who leaves one spouse may do it again; (2) There may be the burden of alimony to the ex-spouse and; (3) If the man doesn't get a divorce and the couple just live together, but later break up or the man dies, the woman will have no rights to alimony or property.

ACTION SECTION

Make a sheet for your Take Charge binder showing the value system you want in a future mate. Don't include such superficial things as wealth or beauty. There are trade-offs in life that make these unimportant. Don't include sexual aspects because nearly all compatible couples have a good sex life. Also leave out things that are selfish, listing only areas where you feel **agreement** is extremely important.

Near the top of a second sheet, enter the behavior pattern that you believe you would like him or her to have, and then list the good features of that behavior pattern. In a second section, list the undesirable features of the pattern you select so you won't be expecting an unreasonable degree of perfection.

The purpose is not to get you to commit yourself, but to make you think about how someone else's values and behavior can affect your future happiness. Be sure to consider how the person you describe will react to your values and behavior. You might find it stimulating to consider pros and cons of several acceptable behaviors.

Don't be afraid to face reality. If you think this a cold blooded approach to love, you may be right. However, remember a house built on a weak foundation will eventually collapse. Love will not overcome all problems in spite of what TV and romantic books lead you to believe.

When the time comes to make a lifetime commitment, you are going to have to accept some characteristics you may feel are negatives, so consider the bad with the good

This photograph of Grandpop and his wife, Susan, reflects 52 years of loving and trusting.

CHAPTER XIV

CONCLUSION

You teen-agers will be the leaders of our nation in years to come. What you do with your lives in the next few years will not only establish the morals and integrity of your lives but also will affect the morals and integrity of our nation.

Generally speaking, people who dedicate their lives to serving others are happier than those who dedicate their lives to self-serving pursuits. Since life is not perfect, everyone will experience some stressful and unpleasant situations. The stress can be reduced by anticipating such situations and by learning to handle people successfully.

The highest-paying jobs are those with the greatest stress caused by others who are self-serving. Examples are legal, executive and administrative jobs. Qualifying for such jobs takes the same commitment and self-discipline that is required to build a happy life.

Teachers, medical, welfare workers, and ministers also have stress filled jobs, but the reward is in the satisfaction and happiness that comes from serving others, not in monetary gain.

We adults have done a poor job of setting good examples for you to follow in building a happy life. If the present trend toward making sexual satisfaction the most important goal in life continues, most of the present problems with crime, drugs, abused children, and venereal diseases will increase manyfold.

Perhaps, you are not convinced that all of these problems are caused by sexual and moral irresponsibility. Logic and looking back at history should convince you.

In the United States, before modern birth prevention methods were developed, there was much less crime. Sex crimes were almost unheard of because people's sexual urges weren't being stimulated by TV, books, and movies. Now we can't build prisons fast enough, and the people don't want to be taxed to pay for them. So, criminals are turned lose to prey on honorable people again and again. Sex crimes are more frequent and many times more horrible.

In China, before Communism, the family was the center of everyone's existence. Members of each family cared for their own. The old folks were honored, and the children were loved and taught. If a child committed an offense, he was disciplined in the family circle.

Many great civilizations, such as the Roman Empire, were destroyed as much by sexual and political irresponsibility from within as they were by barbarian hordes that attacked a weakened nation.

Remember the principle: *LOVE YOUR NEIGHBOR AS YOURSELF.* This doesn't mean romantic love, but concern for the well being of others.

If you believe this book has been helpful to you, keep it handy and reread one chapter on a certain day each month or whenever you are otherwise bored. Write this date on your Take Charge list. This process will keep you on track in your quest for an enjoyable and fun-filled youth.

You have only one body and one lifetime. Use them wisely so you will be free and strong enough to love deeply, openly, joyfully, and permanently.

MAY GOD BLESS YOU AND MAY YOU ENJOY LIFE!

APPENDIX A

PARENTAL INVOLVEMENT IN BUILDING A GOOD LIFE

One of the greatest satisfactions in life is watching a child walk on his own after you have shown him the way.

Parents (and grandparents) love their children and want to give them all of the time and advantages they can afford. They share their children's feelings. They enjoy seeing young people laughing and having fun. They are thrilled and proud when they have successes, such as making the team, being in the school play or being honored for accomplishments.

Happy and successful people are not born. They are the product of loving parents who taught them, nurtured them and gave them a good values system. That system included willingness to accept responsibility for self and consideration for others.

GUIDANCE NEEDED

Developing a sense of responsibility while having fun is largely up to the young people, but it is much easier if parents can find the time to talk with them frequently and to encourage them when they show progress. Good managers and good parents know that development of personal skills is far more important and rewarding than getting a particular physical task completed.

Most parents want to give their children a better life than they had. Sometimes, they give them many material things, and try to protect them from life's pitfalls. Frequently, this is done by busy parents to compensate for lack of personal involvement. It is a sign of love, but not as much as listening and talking to their children.

A far greater gift than too much material help or too much protection is helping them to develop good relationships with people, to accomplish things by themselves, and to accept responsibility for their actions.

In the early teens, when young people are maturing physically, they also are developing stronger wills and emotions. However, they haven't had the experience of their parents in controlling these forces. As a result, they frequently upset parents with their willful and emotional outbursts. Also, as a result, the parents react inappropriately.

To better understand what motivates parents to use an inappropriate method of discipline, let's review typical stages of behavior and discipline as a child increases in age.

Babies are controlled by love, praise and a simple, "No, No." As they grow older, they must be controlled by more forceful means because they are learning to manipulate parents and others. Sometimes, a parent gets so exasperated, he or she yells, threatens, or administers some form of punishment. These steps usually produce results, at least temporarily. Even then, logical choices and rewards work better than confrontation.

When the child reaches the teens, he or she has developed an active mind and conscience and is capable of responding to logic, as well as becoming very emotional. Corporal or other types of punishment build resentment and are not as effective as calm discussion that appeals to the conscience.

Unfortunately, many parents do not sense the extent of the internal emotional development in their teen-agers, so they continue to criticize and yell at the young person who does wrong or is slow to react. They wouldn't do this to a stranger or friend because they know such behavior would create resentment and drive the person away. Yet, they use this method with their children to "save time."

Most parents feel they are doing a good job of raising their children and don't understand what causes a child to misbehave. Some wonder what they did wrong, and others blame the child. Accepting or placing blame solves nothing, but changing methods of disciplining might.

PROBLEMS OUR YOUNG PEOPLE FACE

A good home environment is the best foundation for building a happy and successful life. Conversely, an unstable or unfriendly home environment can cause serious problems. A Gallup Poll, reported by the Associated Press in April 1991, found that 47 percent of children who try or consider suicide blame family problems. Six percent of all teens surveyed had attempted to take their life at least once.

If there is friction in your home, this chapter and some of the thoughts in Chapter Eight may be helpful. Even in the best regulated families, there are ups and downs. Sometimes, young people get into trouble because they failed to follow instructions and warnings. Perhaps they remembered, but were influenced by peer pressure, the desire to be independent, or to have fun.

Parents know their children are facing many temptations every day that their generation did not face, and they can't possibly know everything going on in their children's lives. This is so even when there is time to share and when communication between parent and child is good.

An article in the Wall Street Journal about drug use quoted a father as saying: "I will never fully know why my son got involved in drugs. In my view, there is still a dangerous myth that good kids from good families don't do drugs. My son had his problems, but he was a sensitive, caring and unforgettable young man." The father spent much time and money trying to get his son straightened out, but it was too late. His son died in a drug-related accident.

Contributing to the vulnerability of young people is the increasing number of mothers who are working outside the home and the growth of single-parent homes. As a result, there is too little time for talking with the young people and too much time for the children to be at home unsupervised. Lack of supervision may lead to experimenting with friends in undesirable or harmful activities.

Children of parents who have a good healthy marriage, with the mother usually at home, are also at risk because young people learn from their peers, including those from broken homes. They would rather listen to peers than to parents who are constantly cautioning them about this or that.

Our schools teach students most of the subjects they need to succeed in life. They also teach them biological phases of sex, but few teach value systems that help a young person be happy in a complex world.

Schools are reluctant to take on this chore because a good value system involves religious beliefs and sanctity of marriage. Some contend discussion of these two subjects in schools would violate the Constitutional guarantees of separation of church and state.

Television, movies, and books are giving young people an unrealistic expectation of life, family, and sex that is contrary to what parents would teach if they had the time.

If parents don't get the job done, children are forced to make many everyday decisions based on what they learn from the media and from other young people, whether for good or bad. So what is the solution? This book supplies much needed information to young adults, but parental guidance, love, and understanding also are needed.

PARENTING METHODS

Family psychologists have classified parenting methods as (1) autocratic, (2) permissive, and (3) democratic. The classifications are not absolute, and one parent may use one method while the other parent uses another. Parents tend to follow the method their parents used and taught them by example.

Autocratic parents expect the child to be obedient and do as told without complaining. It is based on the outdated theories, "Spare the rod and spoil the child," and "Do as I say, not as I do." Communication flows down from parent to child with the parent in full control. It can be described as *LIMITS WITHOUT FREEDOM.*

The autocratic method was reasonably effective in pioneer days when there were fewer temptations and mothers were usually available to console and advise.

This method is based on the presumption that young people cannot make good decisions on their own and must be directed and guided continuously. The child is frequently corrected or criticized in such a manner that communication up to parents is limited.

The autocratic parent causes a teen to either become rebellious or to loose initiative and self-respect. It becomes a case of fight or flight.

Those who fight take out their resentment on others further down the pecking order or outside the family. Without being aware of the cause, they frequently show rebellious conduct as a means of asserting independence and they take unnecessary chances when outside of parental control.

Those children who take flight are less willing to assert independence. They wait to be directed before taking action, lest they be criticized. As a result, they lose self-confidence, self-respect, and initiative. Once the restrictive parental yoke is removed, many become hard workers and good citizens, but they seldom have outgoing personalities.

When children of autocratic parents grow up and marry, they have difficulty showing love to their children and mates because their parents seldom demonstrated love and affection to them. When they leave home, they have some resentment and very little love for the parents who may have sacrificed much for them.

Permissive parents protect their children to their maximum ability. They frequently grant the child's requests, even when the child should and could wait on himself or herself or when granting the request could be harmful. They permit the child to eat what and when he or she pleases, and they "pick up" after him or her.

Permissive parents defend the child even when he or she has done wrong. They threaten discipline or punishment frequently, but, rarely, if ever, carry out the threat. Communication is upward to parents with child in control.

A permissive parent permits the child *MAXIMUM FREEDOM WITH MINIMUM LIMITS.* Parents who use this method are demonstrating love by giving, but the method interferes with the natural process of developing self-control and *accepting responsibility* for actions. It also places an excessive burden on parents who try to comply with the child's many requests.

Children of permissive parents have more self-respect than the children of autocratic parents, but have little sense of belonging or cooperation. They tend to be self-centered, manipulative, and less able to handle upsets because they haven't been encouraged to make decisions on their own or to accept responsibility for their actions and misdeeds.

These children usually become takers instead of givers. When they grow up and marry, the marriage may be rocky because love means giving. When they divorce or lose a job, they will move back home because they have learned from experience that their parents will always be there to help.

Demonstrating love means giving of yourself by offering sympathy and comfort. However, it also means forcing children to make choices and accept responsibility for their own well-being, with due consideration for others. This is the method used by democratic parents.

Democratic parents takes the position that everyone in the family has equal rights, freedoms, and responsibilities, but there must be limits on individual freedom for the welfare of the group. As in any democracy, there must be a leader (parent) to make the final decision, if consensus is not possible or practical. More simply, this method constitutes *FREEDOM WITHIN LIMITS.*

Parents using the democratic method encourage independence but acknowledge interdependence with others, including within the family circle.

DEMOCRACY DOESN'T MEAN YOU WILL GET YOUR WAY, BUT YOU WILL GET YOUR SAY. Parents using the democratic method advocate discussion, thought, and understanding and encourage their children to *make choices and accept consequences.* Thus, children develop self-respect, better understanding as to what is expected of them, and a better acceptance of responsibilities.

EFFECTIVE METHODS OF MOTIVATING

Motivation is an inner force that inspires action.   Democratic parents utilize this force to get best results from their children.

Small children want to help and be like Mom or Dad.   They follow and try to help with chores. If allowed to help when young, the development of this natural desire will make it easier to motivate them in their teens.   Conversely, if discouraged when young, it is harder to get them to accept responsibility in later years.   However, if parents *invite* them to help, *talk* to them, *thank* them, *praise* them when warranted and *demonstrate love* by a hug or by words, children of all ages should start cooperating.

Changing long-established behavior is not easy.   It takes persistence, repetition, friendly requests, and invitation.

Make time for your teens.

Make time for social interaction and serious talks with your children.   Find an activity you enjoy doing together and pursue it.   It can be as simple as playing a game together.   If your child initially declines, keep asking.

A game might offer teaching opportunities, such as word games, but should not be one where one or the other wins consistently.   It might be singing, reading, taking a walk, playing ball, or doing a household task together, but not watching TV.   Concentration on the program interferes with good communication.   Simple requests, however, can be made during commercial breaks.

You can use this book or serious magazine articles to open communication.   If you read with your youngster and find a paragraph or section with which you disagree, ask his or her opinion.   It is your privilege to disagree.   Lecturing forcefully, however, builds barriers. Calm discussion gives a child a chance to ask questions and develop a more relaxed relationship with you.

Parental involvement in the reading reinforces and rounds out knowledge when questions arise. What parents tell to, and discuss with, their children bears far more weight in building character than any book ever written.

Listen to your teens

Many parents get frustrated when they try to discuss important matters with their children because the youngsters won't or can't express their feelings. Children like to talk if they feel free to do so. If a teen has felt suppressed by a parent for years, it may take some time to get him or her relaxed in the parent's presence.

A brush-off in an emotional situation can cause a rift that will discourage future communication. If parents are to motivate the inner person, it can be done only by listening and talking calmly. Children will usually listen to their parents if they are treated as equals and as politely as neighbors and friends.

If your child seems to have something on his or her mind and can't get it out, a hug or an arm around the shoulder will help. Or get them to go for a brisk walk with you. Brisk movement helps one become unstuck and promotes release. Avoid acting alarmed. Things that are serious to a youngster may seem minor to you, but avoid making light of a problem.

If a young person gets emotional about something he or she wants or doesn't want to do, firmly and calmly cut off the conversation. Once a person becomes emotional, whether child or adult, that person usually won't listen to or accept logical reasoning. Leave the door open for further discussion.

Remaining calm when others lose control of their emotions sets a good example and leads to more logical talks in the future. Offer alternative solutions, if possible. If your teen-ager wants something you can't afford, suggest ways he or she can earn the money required. He or she will then learn the value of money and labor as well.

Once understanding is achieved, negotiation and compromise are frequently required where compromise is possible. In compromise, no one is totally satisfied, but everyone is generally agreeable to the proposed solution.

Our nation was made great by men who worked together to write a Constitution that was not totally acceptable to anyone, but generally acceptable to all. This same willingness to compromise can make for a happy family life, as well as prepare a young person for a better life outside the family.

Compromising doesn't mean abdicating responsibility. It means discussing the matter to determine the seriousness of the offense and arriving at a solution that is reasonably satisfactory to both parties. It is using the democratic method of parenting, i.e. letting the youngster make choices and accept consequences.

Once a commitment is made, the youth must be held to it. Firmness will usually be effective, but, if the youth tries to renegotiate, appeal to his or her sense of justice. Try saying, "How would you feel if I didn't keep promises I make to you?"

Of course, compromise may not be possible in many cases, such as those where large expenditures are requested, or where there is serious misbehavior. However, compromise is usually possible where privileges or actions are involved,

If calm discussion fails, there is no need to fear saying, "You can't have it (or do it) because I said so." Children also must learn to accept decisions of higher authority.

If you lose your temper and later realize you have been too hard on a youngster, don't let pride keep you from apologizing. Children learn good and bad from examples set by parents. "Making it up to them" as an alternative to an apology doesn't give as clear a signal as a hug and an apology. This doesn't mean totally skipping discipline, but letting them know you love them and want to help them avoid similar incidents in the future.

Dr. Paul W. Swets,* in a book on communicating with teen-agers, reported on a survey of 800 teenagers to determine what they most wanted to hear from their parents. The five answers most often given were the phrases, "I'm proud of you," "I trust you," "You can always come to me with anything and I will be there to listen," "I understand you"(or "I want to understand you)," and, most of all, "I love you."

Remember how much these phrases would have meant to you when you were young? It is easy to forget.

Encourage initiative.

Surveys made by psychologists indicate that giving recognition and showing appreciation are more effective forces for motivating individuals to action than punishment or material rewards.

Praise your children for progress, as well as accomplishments, especially when you know it took considerable effort. Offer them opportunities to do things on their own and challenge them to achieve desirable objectives.

One of the finest pleasures is the proud feeling we get when others, particularly loved ones, enthusiastically cheer us. Praise and recognition

---

* Swets, Paul W. (1988). *How To Talk So Your Teenager Will Listen.* Waco, Tx.. Word Book.

build self-esteem and confidence, especially if it comes from parents.

Children who are taught to think and do things for themselves will make some mistakes. They might even get hurt, but the hurt will heal and they will learn.

Happy families discuss problems with their teen-agers, including financial problems. Consider letting your children participate in setting the family budget. It will teach them the value of money and good habits in controlling it.

Giving children a voice in family problems builds self-esteem and responsibility, whereas children protected from problems will panic or call upon parents when faced with their own troubles later in life. Such discussions also build family unity and togetherness. More importantly, if you confide in them, they will confide in you.

Many businesses solve problems by a process called brain-storming. A group of people get together to define a problem and to arrive at a solution. No one criticizes the proposals. Instead they analyze each and, in the process, arrive at the most practical solution.

This process can be used to develop children's problem-solving abilities, as well as to get them to confide in you. Young people have active imaginations and they enjoy solving problems. If a parent listens and analyzes suggested solutions without criticizing, the young person will feel he is being treated as an adult and will open up. What better way to get them to talk and think? Of course, they also must be cautioned about discussing family affairs outside of the family circle.

DISCIPLINE

This section deals with situations where parents feel the young people are rebellious and uncooperative. Every situation is different, but the following suggestions may be helpful.

The purpose of discipline is to correct undesirable conduct. This can be done most effectively if a way can be found to stir the young person's conscience, rather than criticizing or punishing.

If young people are to be prepared for the realities of life after they leave home, they must gradually be released from restraint and given reasonable freedom (1) to try new experiences, (2) to make their own decisions and (3) to accept the consequences of those decisions.

Effective parents set reasonable limits, apply them consistently and *trust* their children. They avoid overprotection, or the opposite, confrontation. Children who are tightly controlled will rebel, and those who are too loosely controlled will get into trouble frequently.

Criticism

Too frequently, parents get angry with their children when they learn they have experimented with sex, drugs, alcohol, etc. Sometimes, the parent is too busy to discuss the matter, but decides impulsively who is at fault and unfairly criticizes or punishes harshly.

To suppress a strong-willed person by criticism or punishment is much like trying to stop water from flowing by using your hands. The water is going to seek its natural level. You may slow it up, but it will keep flowing. The only way to stop it is at the source, such as a faucet. You can best correct behavior by getting to the conscience and solving the problem at its source.

Criticism forces young people to go underground and avoid talking to parents, lest they be criticized again. Thus, the children continue to learn by experimenting, until finally, they get into more serious trouble. Criticism also destroys self-confidence. This confidence is very much needed if the youngster is to avoid peer pressure and further mistakes.

If you must criticize, criticize gently. Avoid directly criticizing the youngster, such as "You're stupid," Rather, question the behavior, such as "Wasn't that a stupid thing to do?" If your youngster is in trouble, he or she is hurt and frightened and very much needs your sympathy.

Ask questions gently to get the whole story. At this stage in life, calm discussion is most appropriate. There are always two or more sides to a problem, and there are better solutions than direct criticism or severe punishment.

When a teacher disciplines your child, support your child to the extent that you learn the details of the misdeed so you can be fair in any decisions you make with reference to it, but not to the extent he or she can avoid the consequences of his or her misdeeds.

Nothing in this section should be construed as saying, "Never criticize." Constructive criticism is always in order. Criticism is constructive if it suggests a better way to do things.

One effective method of steering young adults away from undesirable behavior is to frequently use the word, "we." For example, "*We* don't belittle those who are less fortunate," or "*We* make it a point to send a thank-you card within 24 hours after *we* receive a gift." The effect is to unite the young person in the family unit and to improve the feeling of togetherness.

Punishment

Some parents feel they can't trust their children because they have lied many times and seldom keep their promises. Punishment usually only makes matters worse. Fear of punishment is what causes the children to be circumspect in the first place, but it doesn't cause them to regret their actions. Instead it causes resentment, especially if they think the punishment exceeds the importance of the misdeed. It makes no difference that the parent feels the punishment was fair.

It may take much effort to get your teen to a point where you feel you can trust him or her. Improved communication should help, but, if there are such strained relations between child and parent that the child won't cooperate, it might be wise to seek counseling.

When a person willingly makes a commitment and feels he or she is being fairly treated, that person will try to keep the commitment and will work harder in the future to prevent problems. It is wise, therefore, to suggest two or more punishments, and ask the young person which would be most appropriate for someone who had committed this offense against him or her. The objective is to stir up the conscience.

He or she will appreciate your desire to be fair and may suggest the least serious punishment. A desire to avoid or minimize punishment is natural, but, if you arouse the young person's conscience, you have made a greater step toward improvement than you would with punishment.

If he or she won't cooperate, don't back off. Waiving discipline will encourage further irresponsibility. Most children want limits. However, they may not admit it because limits restrict freedom.

It is normal for young people to test their parents. Too often parents threaten, but don't carry through. After a few such episodes of discussing, arbitrating, and holding the line on fair discipline, resentment will disappear and you will thereafter get better cooperation.

Mentioning your own embarrassment or shame when your youngster gets into trouble, adds to your teen's feeling of guilt. The youngster is embarrassed enough and will interpret your self-pity as lack of love for him or her.

After a problem is solved, you can sit down together and work out ways to avoid similar problems in the future. Your teen-ager will appreciate your help and love you for it.

Discipline as a team

To be effective, discipline must be fair and consistent with the seriousness of the offense. This is achieved if the parents agree on the discipline. If a child can play one parent against the other, he or she will do so. It then becomes a game in which the child will try to see how much he or she can get away with. In such cases the friction causes an unhappy home situation. It also results in a child who will have less respect for parents who can be manipulated.

To discipline as a team is especially difficult for parents, particularly in a remarriage when the children are those of only one parent. Many parents adjust to each other in day to day living, but are so firm about their own opinions they avoid sharing them to avoid friction.

An open mind, discussion, and agreement are musts in controlling young people. It is better that discipline be too lax or too strict than to have split authority. The good results from agreeing on discipline will justify the effort.

If the parents can't agree on discipline in specific cases, they should agree on dividing responsibility for disciplining by type of misdeed. This avoids discussion on every incident. Both should honor the decision and jointly enforce it. Working together, parents can accomplish much more than when one takes the whole responsibility.

The following quotations from "Active Parenting" by Dr. Michael Popkin* summarize some of the points made in this chapter.

"Parents can help their children learn responsibility by giving them choices to make and then letting them learn through natural and logical consequences of those choices.

"Parenting skills can be divided into two general categories: encouragement skills (those that move the child ahead) and discipline skills (those that set limits or stop the child's movements.)

"The purpose of parenting is to protect and prepare our children to survive and thrive in the kind of society in which they live. The three ingredients for thriving are (1) belonging, (2) learning, and (3) contributing."

****

CHILDREN LEARN WHAT THEY LIVE

If a child lives with criticism, he learns to condemn.
If a child lives with hostility, she learns to fight.
If a child lives with ridicule, he learns to be shy.
If a child lives with shame, she learns to feel guilty.
If a child lives with tolerance, he learns to be patient.
If a child lives with encouragement, she learns confidence.
If a child lives with praise, he learns to appreciate.
If a child lives with fairness, she learns justice.
If a child lives with security, he learns to have faith.
If a child lives with approval, she learns to like herself.
If a child lives with acceptance, and friendship, he learns to find love in the world.

* Popkin, M. H. (1990). *Active Parenting of Teens: Parent's Guide.* Atlanta, Ga. Active Parenting Inc.

TABLE OF PRINCIPLES TO LIVE BY

It is not what you learn or say, but what you do that counts.

When emotion comes in the door, judgment goes out the window.

Knowledge is power.

Self-discipline breeds self-esteem.

A regular schedule and several different exercises are required to develop and maintain a healthy body.

You get out of life what you put into it.

A quitter never wins and a winner never quits.

Boredom indicates an opportunity to improve the quality of life.

Infatuation is an unreasoning passion or attraction.

Love is a strong feeling of affection. It is trusting and unselfish.

True love can exist only between people who are considerate of each other.

Making love is demonstrating affection and giving and sacrificing for the object of your affections.

Jealousy is a manifestation of selfishness, not love.

Sex is not a toy, but a gift for creating life and building happy marriages.

Teenagers are not mature enough to handle emotional aspects and consequences of intimate sexual relationships.

You pay the penalty for a wrong choice whether you made the choice freely or were influenced by someone else.

Girls are more loving and desirous of close relationships than boys.

Boys are naturally agressive and strongly motivated toward sexual indulgence.

No man is an island.

Friendships are important to a happy and successful life.

Dare to be a leader.

I'm sorry", "Please forgive me", and "I forgive you" are powerful phrases for making peace with yourself and others.

To be popular, be kind, friendly, and enthusiastic.

One enemy can do more harm than a hundred friends can do good.

Honor thy father and thy mother.

For a happier home life, accept responsibility

The more love you give, the more you have left.

Honesty is always the best policy.

A handsome or pretty face is made ugly by a foul mouth.

Cigarettes are the calm before a storm of dependency and ill effects.

Better a designated driver than dead or disabled.

Families that pray together, stay together.

Reading develops brain power as well as knowledge.

Love your neighbor as yourself.

Marriages between people madly in love seldom last, but marriages between people quietly in love last forever.

APPENDIX C

MAKING BEHAVIOR CHARTS

The process for making a chart is relatively simple. Answer the 14 easy questions that follow, entering the appropriate numbers on a score sheet. Add the four columns, and divide the totals by 8. Here is a sample score sheet with sample numbers. You need six columns and 20 lines.

Behavior Score Sheet: John Doe

Qu.	Ans.	D	I	S	C
1	Y	9	1		1
2	F	3	3		
3	N	9		1	9
4	(etc. through 14 lines)				
Totals		55	49	32	22

(Divide totals by 8 and adjust to nearest whole number).

		D	I	S	C
Points		7	6	4	3

Questions for Behavior Classification:

INSTRUCTIONS: Enter numbers for the most appropriate answers on the score sheet. After each question there are four choices: YES, FREQUENTLY, RARELY, and NO. Letters and numbers are shown for each answer. The letter indicates a column on the score sheet and the number is a value to be entered in that column. For example D–7 means to enter 7 on the score sheet in column D.

If your answer to a question is "Yes," select the columns and numbers in the "Yes" column . If "No" is the most appropriate answer, select and enter the numbers in the columns listed in the "NO" column below.

	YES	FRQ	RAR	NO
1. Do you frequently lose patience with people who are slow understanding?	D-9	D-7	D-3	D-1
	I-1	I-3	I-7	I-9
	C-1	C-3	C-7	C-9
2. Do you like to plan and organize projects you must do by yourself?	D-1	D-3	D-7	D-9
	I-1	I-3	I-7	I-9
3. When someone gives you a present, do you usually write a thank you note without urging?	D-1	D-3	D-7	D-9
	S-9	S-7	S-3	S-1
	C-9	C-7	C-3	C-1
4. Do you try to do homework at a certain time each day?	S-9	S-7	S-3	S-1
	C-9	C-7	C-3	C-1
5. Do you feel deeply about problems of people you read about?	D-1	D-3	D-7	D-9
	S-9	S-7	S-3	S-1
6. Do you seek out leadership roles or responsibility involving others?	D-9	D-7	D-3	D-1
	I-9	I-7	I-3	I-1
7. Do you like to go to church or Sunday school regularly?	I-9	I-7	I-3	I-1
	S-9	S-7	S-3	S-1
	C-9	C-7	C-3	C-1

	YES	FRQ	RAR	NO
8. Do you get bored quicker than most others?	I-9	I-7	I-3	I-1
	S-9	S-7	S-3	S-1
	C-1	C-3	C-7	C-9
9. Are you comfortable discussing your feelings, such as anger or love, with acquaintances if they ask?	I-9	I-7	I-3	I-1
	S-1	S-3	S-7	S-9
10. When reading or otherwise concentrating, would you choose being interrupted to chat with a friend rather than not being interrupted?	I-9	I-7	I-3	I-1
	C-1	C-3	C-7	C-9
11. If a person who had no right to complain, but would have hurt feelings over something you want to do, would you proceed without further ado?	D-9	D-7	D-3	D-1
	S-1	S-3	S-7	S-9
12. Do you plan or develop schedules for major school projects, such as book reports, to get them in on time?	D-9	D-7	D-3	D-1
	C-9	C-7	C-3	C-1
13, Do you ever do more studying than required to satisfy your curiosity about a subject?	I-1	I-3	I-7	I-9
	S-1	S-3	S-7	S-9
14. If an acquaintance insulted you, would you do unto him what he did to you?	D-9	D-7	D-3	D-1
	C-1	C-3	C-7	C-9

After you have entered all of the numbers on the score sheet, add each column and divide each total by 8.

Entering Patterns On a Behavior Chart

On a 3x5 card, enter numbers 10 through 1 down the left side with columns for D, I, S, and C. Draw a horizontal line across the card between 5 and 6 so you can see whether you score high or low. Then place an X where a number and letter coincide. See the Behavior Chart illustration below to see how D7,I9,S4,2C would be entered.

```
BEHAVIOR CHART FOR _____:

   Score      D       I       S       C
    10
     9                 X
     8
     7         X
     6  _____
     5
     4                         X
     3
     2                                 X
  ___1

 COMMENTS;   His outstanding characteristics are:
 (1) He is an extrovert and gets along well with
 people; and (2) He is impulsive, makes decisions
 quickly and is constantly trying to persuade
 other people to go along with him.    Occasi-
 onally, gets crossed up with school officials."
```

The advantage of using a chart is easy interpretation. For example, a glance at this chart tells you this person is high I and low C, i.e., an outgoing person who is impulsive and who isn't overly concerned with schedules or task completion. The D and S are near average and not as significant.

Without a chart, the letters and numbers must be studied for a minute to come to the same conclusion.

HOTLINE NUMBERS

Check local phone numbers, and local medical clinics, social service agencies, Salvation Army, and YWCA before calling 800 numbers.

SEX-RELATED:
  AIDS Information: 1-800-342-AIDS
  Birthright: Information for pregnant women and assistance to women and couples wishing to keep the baby or arrange adoption.   1-800-848-LOVE.
  Planned Parenthood: Birth Control and Abortion Information   Local number.
  National VD Hotline: (Exc. Calif. 1-800-227-8922 (Calif only) 1-800-982-5883

ALCOHOL:
  Al-Anon Family Support: 1-800-344-2666
        (In New York only)   1-800-245-4656
  National Council on Alcoholism: 1-800-NCA-CALL

DRUGS:
  National Cocaine Hotline: 1-800-COCAINE
  National Inst. on Drug Abuse: 1-800-622-HELP
  PRIDE (Parents Resource Institute for Drug Education):   Local number.

ABUSE AND HOMELESS KIDS:
  Boys Town National: Family crisis hotline. Provides homes for homeless kids   1-800-448-3000
  Covenant House: (Same services as Boys Town)   1-800-999-9999
  National Youth Hotline   1-800-HIT-HOME
  Runaway Hotline: 1-800-231-6946
  Runaway National Switchboard 1-800-621-4000

SUICIDE CONTEMPLATED: Most phone companies render this service. Mention emergency. Get a friend to find an appropriate number if you are depressed.

SPECIAL BOOKLETS (Write for price lists):
Ann Landers   Abigail Van Buren
P. O. Box 11562   P. O. Box 447
Chicago, Ill. 60611-0562   Mt. Morris, Il. 61054

FITNESS PROGRAM FOR TEEN-AGERS

This exercise program doesn't require expensive equipment and can be done at home. It takes only twelve minutes a day and should help you become physically fit without undue strain.

Six of the exercises are for both boys and girls, but there are five more for girls for a more supple body. The goals for girls are lower so all eleven can be done in twelve minutes. However, if girls have the energy and wish to aim for the boy goals, they will add about four minutes to the time.

If you have, or in the recent past, have had indications of physical problems that might cause a strain on heart or lungs, you are advised to consult with your physician or physical education teacher .

People who exercise until exhausted tend to lose interest and quit. Therefore, do not exceed the number of exercises specified for the first fifteen days, but do them every day. It is important that you not do too much. This control also is necessary for developing self-discipline.

A schedule of exercises and goals appears on the next page. The first column of figures is the recommended starting number for each exercise, the second is the goal for the fifteenth day, and the third is the final goal. For the first two weeks, increase the starting number on each third day so you will reach the numbers in the second column on the fifteenth day.

After you reach the 15-day goal, increase the number of each exercise slighty each week thereafter until you reach the final goal. Numbers can be adjusted to fit your skill level. Guard against exceeding the time limit until you reach the final goals in the chart.

	Girls			Boys		
Exercise:	1st	15th	Fin	1st	15th	Fin
Toe Touching	3	8	15	4	10	28
Sit Ups	4	9	27	4	10	28
Chest & Leg Raise	4	14	42	4	14	42
Push Ups	3	8	19	3	8	22
Run In Place	55	70	150	120	245	525
Jumping Jacks	4	8	30	5	30	70
Knee Raising	3	8	22			
Lateral Bending	5	10	14			
Arm Flinging	15	20	30			
Side Leg Raising	4	9	42			
Leg Overs	2	7	13			

EXERCISE CHART

You may substitute jogging or walking for running in place and jumping jacks, but jog for at least fifteen minutes, or walk briskly for thirty minutes. Continue to do the other exercises to strengthen other parts of the body.

Count one each time a left-right movement is completed. Do the exercises daily until you reach the final goal. Then, you may drop back to three sessions per week, or increase each goal. If you wish to lose weight, continue running in place and do jumping jacks for a longer period.

If you decide to set higher goals, check your pulse occasionally to be sure you are not exceeding 24 beats in 10 seconds (144 beats per minute). If your pulse is higher or you can't say three or four words without taking a breath, slow down.

Here is a description of each exercise you may not know about:

Toe Touching: At first, bob a few times without touching floor until muscles are loosened up.

Sit Ups: At first, prop feet under something until you can sit up without using arms.

Chest & Leg Raise: Lay on floor, chest down. At first raise one leg at a time, alternating, and simultaneously raising shoulders off floor so body is resting on stomach. Later, when muscles are better developed, lift both legs and shoulders simultaneously..

Push Ups: At first, push body off floor from knees forward, later from toes forward.

Run In Place: Count one each time left foot touches floor. After each count of fifty for girls, seventy-five for boys, intersperse with ten jumping jacks.

Jumping Jacks: At first, bring arms up to a horizontal position until you can bring hands together.

Knee Raising: Standing, raise left knee, pulling it to chest with hands. Then right knee.

Lateral Bending: Bend sideways to left reaching down with left hand as far as possible with right hand over your head, then repeat for right side.

Arm Flinging: The first two weeks, work your arms like a windmill, half forward and half backward. Thereafter, extend elbows to side, hands on chest, and fling arms backward and up.

Side Leg Raising: Lie on side. Raise one leg to a perpendicular position. Do half left, half right.

Leg Overs: Lie on back, arms straight out. Raise both legs to a perpendicular position. Roll to one side trying to touch toes or legs to the hand on the floor. Then the other side.

REFERENCES

Bradshow, J. (1987). *The Family.* Deerfield Beach, Fla., Health Communication, Inc.

Byrd, R. G. (1988). *Positive Therapeutic Effects of Intercessory Prayer in a Coronary Care Unit Population.* So. Medical Journal, 81(7), 826–829.

Davis, K. (1988). *How To Live With Your Parents Without Losing Your Mind!* Grand Rapids, Mich., Zondervan Pub. House.

Dobson, J. (1978). *Preparing for Adolescence.* Ventura, Ca., Regal Books.

Dobson, J. (1982). *Dr. Dobson Answers Your Questions About Confident Healthy Families* Wheaton, Ill., Tyndale House Publishers, Inc.

Farrell, Warren (1988). *Why Men Are the Way They Are.* New York, Berkley Book.

Howell, J. C. (1973). *Teaching Your Children About Sex.* Nashville, Tn., Broadman Press

Hirsh, S. & Kummerow, J. (1989). *Life Types.* New York, Warner Books, Inc.

Hyde, J. S. (1985). *Half The Human Experience: The Psychology of Women* (3rd Ed.). Lexington, Mass., D. C. Heath & Co.

Lewis, H. (1990). *A Question of Values: Six Ways We Make the Personal Choices That Shape Our Lives.* New York, Harper Collins.

Lewis, P. (1985). *Forty Ways to Teach Your Child Values.* Wheaton, Ill., Tyndale House Publishers.

McDowell, J. *How To Help Your Child say "No" to Sexual Pressure.* Waco, Tex., Word Books.

McDowell, J. *Love Dad--Positive Answers for Teens on Handling Sexual Pressure,* Waco, Tex., Word Books.

Minge, Guiliani & Bowman (1982). *Mating.* Babylon, N.Y., Red Lion Books.

Morris, C. G. (1988). *Psychology: An Introduction.* (6th Ed.). Englewood Cliffs, N.J., Prentice Hall.

Nordberg, M. (1988). *ED Nurses Take A Stand.* Emergwency Medical Services 17-8 p. 20 9–88.

Peterson, E. H. (1987). *Growing Up With Your Teenager.* Old Tappan, N.J., Power Books.

Popkin, M. H. (1990). *Active Parenting of Teens: Parent's Guide.* Atlanta, Ga. Active Parenting Inc.

Popkin, M. H. (1987). *Active Parenting: Teaching, Cooperation, Courage, and Responsibility.* San Francisco, Harper & Row.

Powell, E. (1991). *Talking Back to Sexual Pressure: What To Say.* Minneapolis, Mn., CompCare Publishers.

Swets, Paul W. (1988). *How To Talk So Your Teenager Will Listen.* Waco, Tx., Word Books.

U.S.Dept. of Health & Human Services. *Morbidity & Mortality Weekly Report, Jan. 3 & April 10, 1992.*

U. S. Center For Disease Control (CDC), *Various reports on Condom Use and Use-Effectiveness, HIV/AIDS, Sexual Risk Taking,* Population Report, Sept. 1990, Journal of Adolescent Health 1991, HIV/AIDS Surveillance Report Oct. 1992, et al,

INDEX

BOOK ORDERING INFORMATION

Additional books may be ordered from the following address for $9.95 each plus $2.05 shipping and handling for the first book plus 50 cents for each additional book up to six. Checks, Visa and Master Card accepted.

Please specify Teen Self-Esteem, print your name and address to prevent errors, and specify the Credit Card Company number, and expiration date.

BOOKMASTERS 1444 US Route 42, RD. 11, Mansfield, OH 44903 or Call 1-800-247-6553 or Fax 1-419-281-6883.